THE NOTEBOOK OF
MALTE LAURIDS BRIGGE

The Notebook of
MALTE LAURIDS BRIGGE

Rainer Maria Rilke

TRANSLATED BY
JOHN LINTON

LONDON
THE HOGARTH PRESS
1959

PUBLISHED BY

The Hogarth Press Ltd.

LONDON

This Translation
First published 1930
Reprinted 1950
Reprinted 1959

PART ONE

People come here, then, to live? I should rather
have thought that they came here to die. I have been
out, and I saw hospitals. I saw a poor fellow stagger
and fall. People gathered round him: so I was spared
the rest. I saw a pregnant woman. She dragged herself
heavily along a high, warm wall, now and again grop-
ing for it as if to assure herself it was still there. Yes,
it was still there; and behind it—? I looked for it on
my map of the city: *Maison d'Accouchement*. Right.
They will deliver her; they can do that. Further on,
in the rue Saint-Jacques, an immense building with a
cupola. My map said: *Val de Grâce, hôpital militaire*.
I really did not need this information, but that does
not matter. On every side an odour began to rise from
the street. It was, so far as one could distinguish, a
smell of iodoform, the grease of pommes frites, and
fear. Every city has its summer smell. Then I saw a
house curiously blind as if with cataract. It was not to
be found on my map; but above the door there stood
an inscription still fairly readable: *Asile de nuit*. Beside

3

the entrance was the list of charges. I read it. The place was not dear.

And what else? A baby in a perambulator standing on the pavement. The child was stout, of a greenish complexion, and it had a noticeable eruption on its forehead. This was evidently healing and not causing any pain. The child was sleeping with open mouth, breathing iodoform, pommes frites, and fear. This, then, is what it came to. The chief thing was to keep on living. That was the chief thing.

*

To THINK that I cannot give up the habit of sleeping with an open window! The electric street-cars rage through my room with ringing fury. Automobiles race over me. A door slams. Somewhere a window-pane falls clattering. I can hear the big splinters laughing and the smaller ones sniggering. Then suddenly from the other side, within the house, a dull, muffled noise. Someone is coming up the stairs: is drawing nearer and nearer, interminably: is there, there for a long while, then passes. And once more the street. A girl screams: "*Ah! tais-toi, je ne veux plus.*" An electric car rushes up excitedly, then away overhead, away over everything. Someone is calling. People are running, overtaking each other. A dog barks. What a relief: a dog! Towards morning even a cock crows; and that brings immeasurable solace. Then all at once I fall asleep.

*

THESE are the noises. But there is something here that is more terrible: the silence. I believe that in the course of great conflagrations there sometimes occurs a moment of extreme tension: the jets of water fall back; the firemen no longer mount their ladders; no one stirs. Noiselessly a black cornice thrusts itself forward overhead, and a high wall, behind which the flames shoot up, leans forward, noiselessly. All stand motionless and await, with shoulders raised and brows contracted, the awful crash. The silence here is like that.

*

I AM learning to see. I do not know why it is, but everything penetrates more deeply within me and no longer stops at the place, where until now, it always used to finish. I possess an inner self of which I was ignorant. Everything now passes in thither. What happens there I know not.

Today while writing a letter I was struck by the fact that I had been here only three weeks. Three weeks elsewhere — in the country, for example — would be like a day; here they seem like years. And I mean to write no more letters. What would be the good of telling anyone that I am changing? If I am changing, then surely I am no longer the person I was, and if I am someone else than heretofore, then it is clear that I have no acquaintances. And to strangers, to people who do not know me, it is impossible for me to write.

*

Have I said it before? I am learning to see. Yes, I am beginning. It still goes slowly; but I intend to make the most of my time.

For one thing, it has never occurred to me before how many different faces there are. There are quantities of people, but there are even more faces, for each person has several. There are some who wear the same face for years: naturally it wears out; it gets dirty; it splits at the folds; it stretches, like gloves one has worn on a journey. These are thrifty, simple folk; they do not change their face; they never even have it cleaned. It is good enough, they say, and who can prove the contrary? The question of course arises, since they have several faces, what do they do with the others? They keep them. Their children will wear them. But sometimes, too, it happens that their dogs go out with them on. And why not? Faces are faces.

There are others who change their faces in uncannily rapid succession, and wear them out. At first they think they have enough to last them forever; but they have scarcely reached forty when behold, they have come to the last of them. This naturally leads to tragedy. They are not accustomed to being frugal with faces. Their last is worn through in a week, has holes in it, and in many places is as thin as paper; and then gradually the lining — the no-face — comes through, and they go about with that.

But the woman, the woman: she had completely sunk into herself, her head in her hands. It was at the corner of the rue Notre-Dame-des-Champs. I began to walk softly as soon as I saw her. When poor people are reflecting they should not be disturbed. Perhaps what they are seeking will yet occur to them.

The street was too empty; its emptiness was bored with itself; it caught my step from under my feet and clattered about with it hither and yon, as with a wooden clog. The woman took fright and was torn too quickly out of herself, too violently, so that her face remained in her two hands. I could see it lying in them, its hollow form. It cost me an indescribable effort to keep my eyes on these hands and not to look at what had been torn out of them. I shuddered to see a face thus from the inside, but I was still more afraid of the naked, flayed head without a face.

*

I AM afraid. One has to take some action against fear when once it lays hold of one. It would be dreadful to fall ill here, and if it occurred to anyone to take me to the Hôtel-Dieu I should certainly die there. It is very comfortable, this Hôtel, with an enormous clientèle. One can scarcely examine the façade of the Cathedral of Paris without danger of being run over by one of the many vehicles that must make haste across the open square to get in yonder as quickly as possible. They are small omnibuses that sound their bells incessantly, and the Duke of Sagan himself would have to bring his equipage to a halt, if some insignificant person on the point of death had taken it into his head to be borne thus straightway to the Hotel of God. Dying people are headstrong, and all Paris has to slow down when Madame Legrand, brocanteuse from the rue des Martyrs, comes driving in the direction of a certain city square. It is to be noted that these confounded little carriages are provided with extraordinarily intriguing windows of opaque glass behind which one can picture the most magnificent agonies. The imagination of a concierge is enough for that; but if one has a little more inventive power and allows it to develop in other directions, conjecture becomes utterly boundless. But I have also seen open cabs arriving, hired cabs with their hoods folded back, plying for the usual fare: two francs each hour of agony.

*

THIS excellent Hôtel is very ancient. Even in King Clovis' time people died there in a number of beds. Now they are dying there in five hundred and fifty-nine beds. Of course the whole business is mechanical. With such an enormous output an individual death is not so thoroughly carried out; but that is, after all, of little consequence. It is quantity that counts. Who cares anything today for a well-finished death? No one. Even wealthy people who could afford this luxury are beginning to be careless and indifferent about the matter. The desire to have a death of one's own is growing more and more rare. In a little while it will be as rare as a life of one's own. Heavens! it is all there. We come and find a life ready for us: we have only to put it on. We go when we wish or when we are compelled to. Above all, no effort. *Voilà votre mort, monsieur.* We die as best we can; we die the death that belongs to the disease from which we suffer (for since we have come to know all diseases, we know, too, that the different lethal endings belong to the diseases and not to the people; and the sick person has, so to speak, nothing to do).

In sanatoria, where people die so willingly and with so much gratitude to doctors and nurses, they die from one of the deaths assigned to the institution; that is regarded very favourably. But when one dies at home, it is natural to choose that polite and genteel death, with which, as it were, a first-class funeral, with the whole sequence of its beautiful rites, begins. Poor folk stand outside a house where this has taken place and surfeit themselves with the spectacle. Their death is, of course, banal, entirely without formalities. They are glad when they find one that fits approximately. No matter if it is too large; people are always growing a little. The trouble comes when it does not meet round the chest, or when it strangles.

*

WHEN I go back in thought to my home, where there is no one left now, I imagine that formerly things must have been otherwise. Formerly we knew (or perhaps we just guessed) that we carried our death within us, as a fruit bears its kernel. Children had a little death within them, older people a large one. Women had theirs in their womb, men theirs

9

in their breast. One *had* it, and that gave one a singular dignity, a quiet pride.

It was evident that my grandfather, old Chamberlain Brigge, carried his death within him. And what a death it was! It was two months long and so loud that it could be heard as far off as the manor-farm.

The long, old manor-house was too small to hold this death. It seemed as if additional wings would have to be built on it, for the chamberlain's body grew larger and larger, and he continually wanted to be carried from one room to another, falling into a terrible rage when, though the day had not yet come to an end, there was not a room left in which he had not already lain. Then the whole troop of men-servants, maids and dogs, that he always had about him, had to go with him upstairs, under the marshalling of the major-domo, into the room in which his saintly mother had died. It had been kept exactly as she had left it twenty-three years before, and since then no one had ever been allowed to set foot in it. Now the whole pack burst in. The curtains were drawn back, and the robust light of a summer afternoon inspected all the shy, frightened furniture and moved clumsily around in the hastily uncovered mirrors. And the people did the same. There were chamber-maids who, in their curiosity, knew not where their hands were actually straying, young men-servants who gaped at everything, and older retainers who moved to and fro trying to recollect all that had been told them about this sealed room in which they now so fortunately found themselves.

But the dogs especially seemed to find their sojourn, in a room where everything had an odour, extraordinarily exciting. The huge, lean Russian wolfhounds ran busily here and there behind the armchairs, crossed the floor in long dance-steps with a swinging movement, or stood up like heraldic animals, resting their slender paws on the white-and-gold window-sill, and, directing their pointed, expectant muzzles and wrinkled foreheads now to the right, now to the left, looked out into the courtyard. Some small dachshunds, the colour of brownish-yellow glove leather, sat in a large silk-upholstered easy-chair near the window, looking as though everything were quite normal, and a wiry-haired, surly-looking pointer, rubbed his back along the edge of a gilt-legged table, causing the Sèvres cups on its painted surface to tremble.

Yes, for these drowsy, absent-minded objects it was a terrible time. From books hastily opened by some careless hand rose-leaves tumbled and were trampled underfoot; small fragile ornaments were seized, and, immediately broken, were quickly put back again; many, too, were hidden, thrust beneath the curtains, or even flung behind the gilt net-work of the fire-screen. From time to time something fell, fell muffled on the carpet, fell clear on the hard parquetry, but breaking here and there, with a brittle snap or almost inaudibly; for these objects, spoiled as they were, could not survive any sort of fall.

And had it occurred to anyone to ask what caused all this, what had called down upon this jealously guarded room the full measure of destruction, there would have been but one answer: Death.

The death of the chamberlain Christoph Detlev Brigge at Ulsgaard. For he lay on the floor in the middle of the room, swelling enormously out of his dark blue uniform, and never stirred. In his large, strange countenance which no one any longer recognised, the eyes had closed: he saw not what was happening. They had tried at first to lay him on the bed, but this he had resisted, for he detested beds since those nights in which his illness had first grown upon him. Besides, the bed in this upstairs room had proved too small, so nothing remained but to lay him thus upon the carpet; for downstairs again he had refused to go.

So now he lay there, and one might think that he had died. As it slowly began to grow dark, the dogs had slipped away, one after the other, through the half-open door. Only the stiff-haired pointer with the surly face sat beside his master, and one of his broad, shaggy forepaws lay on Christoph Detlev's big, grey hand. Most of the servants, too, were now standing outside in the white-painted corridor, which was brighter than the room; but those who still remained within glanced stealthily now and then at the great darkening heap in the middle, and they wished that it were nothing more than a large garment covering a decayed thing.

But there was something else. There was a voice, that voice which for seven weeks now no one had recognised; for it was not the voice of the chamberlain.

Not to Christoph Detlev did this voice belong, but to Christoph Detlev's death.

For many, many days now Christoph Detlev's death had been living at Ulsgaard, spoke to everyone and demanded: demanded to be carried, demanded the blue chamber, demanded the little drawing-room, demanded the large reception-room. It demanded the dogs, demanded that people should laugh and talk, should play and be quiet, and all at the same time. It demanded to see friends, women and people who were dead, and demanded to die itself: demanded. Demanded and shouted.

For when night had fallen, and those of the over-wearied domestics who were not on duty tried to snatch some sleep, then Christoph Detlev's death shouted, shouted and groaned. It roared so long and so constantly that the dogs, at first howling in concert, were struck dumb and did not dare lie down, but stood on their long, slender, trembling legs, in terror. And when the villagers heard it roaring through the spacious, silvery Danish summer night, they rose from their beds as if there were a thunder-storm, put on their clothes and remained sitting in silence round the lamp until it was over. And women near their time were consigned to the most remote rooms and the most thickly partitioned recesses. But they heard it; they heard it, as if it had cried from their own bodies, and they pled to be allowed to get up too, and came, voluminous and white, to sit with their vacant faces among the others. And the cows that were calving at that time were impotent and bound; one of them had its dead fruit dragged out of its body along with all the entrails, as it simply would not come forth. And all the men on the estate did their daily work badly, and forgot to take in the hay, for throughout the day they dreaded the coming of the night, and they were so worn out by their continuous watchings and terrified awakenings that they could not attend to anything. And when they went on Sundays to the white, peaceful church, they prayed that there might no longer be a master at Ulsgaard; for this was a dreadful master. And the pastor gave utterance from his pulpit to the thoughts and prayers of all; for he also had no nights and could no longer understand God. The bell, too, repeated it; for it had found a terrible rival that boomed the whole night through, a rival against which it could do nothing, even though it took to sounding with all its metal. Indeed, they all said it; and there was one among the younger men who dreamed that he had gone to the manor-house and killed the master with his pitch-fork; and there was so much irritation, exasperation and feverish excitement, that they all listened as he told his dream, and quite unconsciously glanced at him to see if he were really capable of such a deed. That was how people felt and spoke throughout the whole district where, only a few weeks before, the chamberlain had still been loved and pitied. But, though there was all this talk, nothing changed. Christoph Detlev's death, which dwelt at Ulsgaard, was not to be hurried. It had come to stay for ten weeks, and for ten weeks it stayed. And during that time it was more master than ever Christoph Detlev Brigge had been; it was like a king who, afterward and forever, is known as "the Terrible."

Nor was it the death of any mere dropsical sufferer; it was the sinister, princely death which the chamberlain had carried within him and had himself nourished during his whole life. All the superfluous pride, will and mastery he had been unable to consume even in his peaceful days, had passed into his death, that death which now sat and squandered these things at Ulsgaard.

How the chamberlain would have looked at anyone who asked him to die any other death than this! He was dying his own hard death.

*

AND when I think of the others whom I have seen or about whom I have heard, it is always the same. They have all had a death of their own. Those men who carried theirs within their armour, like a prisoner; those women who grew very old and small, and then on a huge bed, as on a stage, passed away, discreet and dignified, in the presence of the whole family, the servants and the dogs. Children, too, even the very little ones, did not die just any kind of childish death; they gathered themselves together and died as that which they already were, and as that which they would have become.

And what a melancholy beauty came to women when they were pregnant, and stood, their slender hands involuntarily resting on their big bodies which bore two fruits: a child and a death. Did not the broad, almost nourishing smile on their quite vacant faces come from their sometimes thinking that both these fruits were growing?

*

I HAVE taken action against fear. I sat up the whole night and wrote; and now I am as thoroughly tired as after a long walk in the fields at Ulsgaard. Still it is bitter for me to think that all that is no more, that strangers live in the old, long manor-house. It may be that in the white room up in the gable the maids are now sleeping, sleeping their heavy, moist sleep from evening until morning.

And one has nothing and nobody, and one travels about the world with a trunk and a case of books, and really without curiosity. What sort of a life is it really: without a house, without inherited possessions, without dogs? If only one had one's memories! But who has them? If one could bring one's childhood to mind— but it is as though it had been buried. Perhaps one must be old to be able to reach back to all that. I think it must be good to be old.

*

TODAY we had a lovely autumn morning. I passed through the Tuileries. Everything that lay towards the East, before the sun, shone with a dazzling light.

The part on which the sun fell was hung with mist, as if with a grey curtain of light. Grey against grey, the statues sunned themselves in the still shrouded gardens. In the long parterres, here and there single flowers stood up and said Red' with a frightened voice. Then a very tall, slim man came round the corner from the Champs Elysées. He carried a crutch; but it was not thrust under his shoulder; he held it lightly in front of him, and from time to time struck it firmly and loudly on the ground, like a herald's staff. He could not repress a smile of joy, and smiled at everything as he passed, at the sun, at the trees. His step was timid as a child's, but unusually light, charged with memories of earlier walking days.

*

How much such a little moon can do! There are days when everything about us is lucent and ethereal, scarcely outlined in the luminous atmosphere and yet distinct. The nearest objects take on the tones of distance, are remote and merely displayed from afar, not given to us. And everything suggestive of spaciousness — the river, the bridges, the long streets, and the lavish squares — has put that spaciousness behind itself, is painted on it as on a tissue of silk. It is not possible to say what a bright green carriage on the Pont Neuf can then become, or a splash of red so vivid that it will not be suppressed, or even a simple placard on the party wall of a pearl-grey group of houses. Everything is simplified, brought into a few, correct, clear planes, like the face in a Manet portrait. And nothing is insignificant or superfluous. The booksellers on the Quai open their stalls, and the fresh or tarnished yellow of their books, the violet brown of the bindings, and the more assertive green of an album — everything harmonises, has value, takes part in creating a fulness in which nothing is lacking.

*

IN the street below there is the following group: a small, double wheelbarrow pushed by a woman; lengthwise across the front of it, a hand-organ; across it at the back, a basket in which a quite young child is standing on firm legs, happy beneath its cap, not wanting to be made to sit. From time to time the woman turns the handle of the organ. Then the child immediately gets up again, stamping in its basket, while a little girl in a green Sunday dress dances and beats a tambourine uplifted towards the windows.

*

I THINK I ought to begin to do some work, now that I am learning to see. I am twenty-eight years old, and almost nothing has happened. Let us recall what I have done. I have written a study on Carpaccio which is bad, a drama entitled 'Marriage,' which sets out to demonstrate a false thesis by dubious means, and some verses. Ah! but verses amount to so little when one begins to write them young. One ought to wait and gather sense and sweetness a whole life long, and a long life if possible, and then, quite at the end, one might perhaps be able to write ten good lines. For verses are not, as people imagine, simply feelings (we have these soon enough); they are experiences. In order to write a single verse, one must see many cities, and men and things; one must get to know animals and the flight of birds, and the gestures that the little flowers make when they open out to the morning. One must be able to return in thought to roads in unknown regions, to unexpected encounters, and to partings that had been long foreseen; to days of childhood that are still indistinct, and to parents whom one had to hurt when they sought to give one some pleasure which one did not understand (it would have been a pleasure to someone else); to childhood's illnesses that so strangely begin with such a number of profound and grave transformations, to days spent in rooms withdrawn and quiet, and to mornings by the sea, to the sea itself, to oceans, to nights of travel that rushed along loftily and flew with all the stars — and still it is not enough to be able to think of all this. There must be memories of many nights of love, each one unlike the others, of the screams of women in labour, and of women in childbed, light and blanched and sleeping, shutting themselves in. But one must also have been beside the dying, must have sat beside the dead in a room with open windows and with fitful noises. And still it is not yet enough to have memories. One must be able to forget them when they are many and one must have the immense patience to wait until they come again. For it is the memories themselves that matter. Only when they have turned to blood within us, to glance and gesture, nameless and no longer to be distinguished from ourselves — only then can it happen that in a most rare hour the first word of a poem arises in their midst and goes forth from them.

But all my verses had a different origin; so they are not verses. And when I wrote my drama, how far astray I went! Was I an imitator and a fool that I needed to introduce a third person in order to describe the fate of two human beings who made life hard for one another? How easily I fell into the trap! And I ought nevertheless to have known that this third person who pervades all life and literature, this ghost of a third person who has never existed, has no significance and must be disavowed. He is one of the pretexts of Nature who is always endeavouring to divert the attention of men from her deepest secrets. He is the screen behind which a drama is unfolded. He is the noise at the threshold of the voiceless stillness of a real conflict. One is inclined to say that heretofore every writer has found it too difficult to speak of the two in question. The third, just because he is so unreal, is the easiest part of the undertaking; him they can all manage. From the very beginning of their plays one notices their impatience to arrive at this third person; they can scarcely wait for him. The moment he appears all is well. But how tiresome when he is late! Absolutely nothing can happen without him; everything stops, hesitates, waits. Yes, and how if this delay and obstruction were to continue? What, sir dramatist, and you, enlightened public that knows life, what if he were proclaimed missing, this popular man-about-town or this arrogant youth, who fits into every marriage like a master-key? What if, for example, the devil took him? Let us assume this. All at once the theatres are seen to become unnaturally empty; they are bricked up like dangerous holes; only the moths from the rims of the boxes tumble through the vacant hollow space. The dramatists no longer enjoy their villas in the residential quarter. All the public detective agencies are employed in searching on their behalf for the indispensable third person who was the essence of the action.

And all the time they are living amongst us — not these 'thirds' but the other two, about whom such an incredibly great deal might be said, about whom nothing has ever been said hitherto, although they suffer and act and know not how to help themselves.

It is laughable. Here I sit in my little room, I, Brigge, who have grown to be eight-and-twenty years old and of whom no one knows. I sit here and am nothing. And nevertheless this nothing begins to think and, five flights up, on a grey Parisian afternoon, thinks these thoughts:

Is it possible, it thinks, that nothing real or important has yet been seen or known or said? Is it possible that mankind has had thousands of years in which to observe, reflect and record, and has allowed these millennia to slip past, like a recess interval at school in which one eats one's sandwich and an apple?

Yes, it is possible.

Is it possible that despite our discoveries and progress, despite our culture, religion and world-wisdom, we still remain on the surface of life? Is it possible that we have even covered this surface, which might still have been something, with an incredibly uninteresting stuff which makes it look like drawing-room furniture during summer holidays?

Yes, it is possible.

Is it possible that the whole history of the world has been misunderstood? Is it possible that our conception of the past is false, because we have always spoken of its masses, as though we were telling of a vast aggregation of human beings, instead of about the One around whom they gathered because he was a stranger and was dying?

Yes, it is possible.

Is it possible that we have believed it necessary to recover what happened before we were born? Is it possible that every individual has had to be reminded that he is indeed sprung from all those who have gone before, that he has known this therefore and ought not to have been persuaded differently by others who knew otherwise?

Yes, it is possible.

Is it possible that all these people know with perfect accuracy a past that has never existed? Is it possible that all realities are nothing to them, that their life runs on, unconnected with anything, like a watch in an empty room — ?

Yes, it is possible.

Is it possible that we know nothing of young girls who nevertheless live? Is it possible that we say 'women,' 'children,' 'boys,' not guessing (despite all our culture, not guessing) that these words have long since had no plural, but only countless singulars?

Yes, it is possible.

Is it possible that there are people who speak of 'God' and mean something they have in common? Take a couple of schoolboys: one buys a pocket knife and his companion buys another exactly like it on the same day. And after a week they compare knives and find that there is now only a very distant resemblance between them — so different has been their lot in different hands. ('Well,' says the mother of one of them, 'if you always must wear everything out immediately —') Ah, then is it possible to believe that one can have a God without using Him?

Yes, it is possible.

But if all this is possible — has even no more than a semblance of possibility — then surely, for all the world's sake, something must be done. The first comer, he who has had these disturbing thoughts, must begin to do some of the neglected things; even if he be just anybody, by no means the most suitable person: there is no one else at hand. This young, insignificant foreigner, Brigge, will have to sit down in his room five flights up and write, day and night. Yes, he will have to write; that will be the end of it.

*

TWELVE years old, or at most thirteen, I must have been at the time. My father had taken me with him to Urnekloster. I do not know what occasion he had to look up his father-in-law. Since my mother's death many years before, the two men had not seen each other, and my father himself had never been in the old manor-house to which Count Brahe had but recently retired. I never again saw that remarkable house, which after my grandfather's death passed into strange hands. So far as I can recover it in the recollections of my childhood, it is not a complete building; it is all broken up in my memory, a room here, and a room there, and then part of a hallway that does not connect these two rooms but is preserved as a fragment by itself. In this way it is all dispersed within me — the rooms, the stairways that descended with such ceremonious deliberation, and other narrow, corkscrew stairs in the obscurity of which one moved as blood does in the veins; the tower rooms, the lofty, suspended balconies, the unexpected, balustraded galleries onto which you were thrust out through a little door — all that is still in me and will never cease to be in me. It is as though the picture of this house had fallen into me from an immeasurable height, and had been shattered on my inmost being.

There remains whole in my heart, so it seems

to me, only that large hall in which we used to gather for dinner every evening at seven o'clock. I never saw this room in daytime; I do not even remember whether it had windows or on what they looked out; whenever the family entered, the candles were lit in the ponderous branched candlesticks, and in a few minutes one forgot the time of day and all that one had seen outside. This lofty and, as I suspect, vaulted chamber was stronger than all else. With its crepuscular height and its corners that were never quite illumined, it sucked all the ideas out of you without giving you anything positive in exchange for them. You sat there as if dissolved — entirely without will, without intelligence, without desire, defenceless. You were like a vacant place. I remember that at first this state of annihilation made me almost ill; it brought on a kind of sea-sickness which I only overcame by stretching out my leg until I touched with my foot the knee of my father who sat opposite me. It did not strike me until afterwards that he seemed to understand, or at least to tolerate, this singular behaviour, albeit there existed between us an almost cool relationship which would not account for such a gesture. Nevertheless it was this slight contact that gave me strength to support these long repasts. And after a few weeks of spasmodic endurance, I became, with the almost boundless adaptability of children, so inured to the eeriness of these gatherings, that it cost me no effort to remain at table for two hours. The time even passed comparatively swiftly, for I occupied myself in observing those present.

My grandfather called them 'the family,' and I also heard the others use the same designation, which was entirely arbitrary. For, although these four persons were remotely akin to one another, they in no way belonged together. My uncle, who sat next me, was an old man, on whose hard, sun-burned countenance there were some black spots, the result, as I learned, of a powder-explosion. Morose and soured, he had retired from the army with the rank of major, and now employed himself in making alchemistic experiments in some region of the manor-house unknown to me; was also, as I heard the servants say, in communication with a prison whence once or twice a year corpses were sent him with which he shut himself in night and day, and which he cut up and prepared in some mysterious fashion so that they withstood putrefaction. Opposite him was the place of Fräulein Mathilde Brahe. She was a person of uncertain age, a distant cousin of my mother's. Nothing was known of her beyond the fact that she kept up a very industrious correspondence with an Austrian spiritualist who called himself Baron Nolde, and to whom she was so completely submissive that she would not undertake the slightest thing without first securing his consent, or rather, something like his benediction. She was at that time exceptionally robust, and had a soft, lazy amplitude that looked as if it had been carelessly poured into her loose and gaudy clothes. Her movements were tired and undecided, and her eyes watered continually. Despite that, there was something about her which reminded me of my frail, slender mother. The longer

I looked at her, the more I found in her face all those delicate and gentle features which since my mother's death I had never been able rightly to recall; only now, since I was seeing Mathilde Brahe every day, did I know again how my dead mother looked; indeed, perhaps I knew it for the first time. Now for the first time did the hundreds and hundreds of details compose in me an image of her who was dead, that image which accompanies me everywhere. Afterwards it became clear to me that in Fräulein Brahe's face were actually present all the details which determined my mother's features — only they looked as if some strange face had thrust itself among them, separated, warped, and no longer connected with each other.

Beside this lady sat the little son of a female cousin, a boy of about the same age as myself, but smaller and more delicate. His pale, lean neck rose out of a pleated ruff, and disappeared beneath a long chin. His lips were thin and tightly shut, his nostrils trembled slightly, and of his fine, dark-brown eyes only one was moveable. It often sent across to me a quiet and melancholy look, while the other always remained fixed on one point as though it had been disposed of and need no longer be taken into account.

At the head of the table stood my grandfather's huge arm-chair, which a man-servant, who had nothing else to do, pushed beneath him, and in which the old man took up very little room. There were people who called this deaf and masterful old gentleman 'Excellency' or 'Marshal,' while others gave him the title of 'General.' And he doubtless possessed all these dignities; but it was so long since he had held any office that such appellations were hardly intelligible any more. It seemed to me as if no definite name could be attached anyway to this personality, at certain moments so keen, yet always turning vague again. I could not make up my mind to call him Grandfather, albeit he was occasionally quite friendly to me; indeed he sometimes even called me to him, endeavouring withal to give a playful intonation to my name. Besides, the attitude of the whole family towards the Count was one of mingled veneration and timidity. Little Erik alone lived in any degree of intimacy with the old master of the house. His moveable eye at times shot him rapid glances of understanding to which Grandfather responded with equal rapidity. Sometimes, too, on the long afternoons one might see them appear at the end of the long gallery, and observe how they walked, hand in hand, past the sombre old portraits, without speaking, apparently understanding one another in some other way.

I spent nearly the whole day in the park and outside in the beech-groves or on the heath. Fortunately there were dogs in Urnekloster to accompany me. Here and there I would come across a tenant's house, or a farmsteading, where I could get milk and bread and fruit. I believe I was, to a large extent, care-free in the enjoyment of my liberty, and did not allow myself, at least in the weeks that followed, to be troubled by the thought of the evening gatherings. I scarcely spoke to anyone, for it was my delight to be alone; only with the dogs I had short conversations now and again:

we understood one another admirably. Taciturnity was moreover a kind of family characteristic. I was accustomed to it in my father, and it did not surprise me that there was almost no conversation at dinner.

Still, during the early days of our visit, Mathilde Brahe showed herself extremely talkative. She asked my father about old acquaintances in foreign cities; she recalled bygone impressions, even moved herself to tears by evoking the memory of departed friends and of a certain young man, who, she hinted, had been in love with her though she had not been able to respond to his pressing but hopeless passion. My father listened politely, bending his head now and again in agreement, and answering only when necessary. The Count, at the head of the table, sat with a perpetual smile on his lips which were drawn down in contempt; his face seemed larger than usual, as though he were wearing a mask. He also frequently joined in the conversation himself, without directing his remarks to anyone in particular; but though his voice was very low it could nevertheless be heard through the whole room. It had something of the regular, indifferent movement of a pendulum; the silence around it seemed to have a strange, empty resonance, the same for every syllable.

Count Brahe thought he did my father an especial courtesy in speaking to him of his deceased wife, my mother. He called her the Countess Sibylle, and all his sentences finished as if he were enquiring after her. Indeed it appeared to me, I know not why, as if he were speaking of some very young girl in a white dress, who might appear amongst us at any moment. I heard him speak, too, in the same tone of 'our little Anna Sophie.' And when one day I asked who this young damsel was, of whom my grandfather seemed so particularly fond, I discovered that he meant the daughter of the High Chancellor Conrad Reventlov, the whilom morganatic wife of Frederick the Fourth, who for nearly a hundred and fifty years had been reposing at Roskilde. The passing of time had absolutely no significance for him, death was a trifling incident which he utterly ignored, persons whom he had once received into his memory continued to exist and their dying could not alter that in the least. Several years later, after the old gentleman's death, they would tell how he had persisted with the same obstinacy in treating future things as present. He was said to have spoken on one occasion to a certain young, married lady about her sons, in particular about the travels of one of them, while she, being just in the third month of her first pregnancy, sat almost insensible with horror and fright as the old man talked incessantly on.

But the thing began with my laughing. Indeed, I laughed out loud and could not stop myself. One evening Mathilde Brahe was not present. In spite of that, the aged, almost stone-blind servitor held out the dish when he came to her seat. He remained in that attitude for a little, then, placid and dignified and as if all were in order, he went on. I had watched this scene, and for the moment, as I looked, it did not seem at all funny. But shortly after, just as I was about to swallow a mouthful of food, a fit of laughter seized me so suddenly that I choked and made a great noise. And though the situation was painful for me and I made every possible effort to be serious, the impulse to laugh recurred spasmodically and completely dominated me.

My father, as if to screen my bad manners, asked in his broad, subdued tones, 'Is Mathilde ill?' My grandfather smiled his peculiar smile and answered in a sentence to which, taken up with myself as I was, I paid no attention, but which sounded something like this:

'No, she merely does not wish to meet Christine.'

Neither did I notice, therefore, that it was these words which made my neighbour, the swarthy major, rise and, with an indistinctly muttered apology and a bow in the Count's direction, leave the room. It only struck me when he turned once more at the door, behind the back of the master of the house, and made nodding and beckoning signs to little Erik and suddenly, to my great astonishment, to me as well, as though he were ordering us to follow him. I was so surprised that my laughter ceased to press upon me. Beyond that I paid no further attention to the major; I thought him unpleasant, and I noticed, too, that little Erik took no notice of him.

The meal dragged on as usual, and we had just reached the dessert when my eye was caught and held by a movement going on in the dim light at the back of the room. In that quarter a door which I thought was always kept shut, and which I had been told led to the mezzanine floor, had been gradually opened, and now, as I looked on with a feeling entirely new to me of curiosity and amazement, there stepped into the darkness of the doorway, a slender, gaily-clad lady, who came slowly towards us. I do not know whether I made any movement or sound; the noise of a chair being overturned forced me to tear my eyes from that strange apparition, and I caught sight of my father, who had leaped up and now, his face the colour of death, and his hands clenched by his sides, was going towards the lady. Quite unmoved by this spectacle, she walked towards us, step by step, and was already close to the Count's place, when he rose brusquely and, seizing my father by the arm, drew him back to the table and kept hold of him; while the strange lady passed slowly and indifferently through the space now left clear, moving step by step, through an indescribable stillness, in which only the trembling rattle of a glass sounded, and disappeared through a door in the opposite side of the room. At that moment I observed that it was little Erik who, with a profound obeisance, closed the door behind the stranger.

I was the only one who had remained seated at the table. I felt so heavy in my chair that it seemed to me as if I could never get up again by myself. For a while I stared without seeing. Then I thought of my father, and became aware that the old man still held him by the arm. My father's face was now furious and swollen with blood, but Grandfather, whose fingers were clutching his arm like a white claw, still smiled his mask-like smile. Then I heard him say something, catching each syllable, but unable to understand the meaning of his words. They must nevertheless have made a profound impression on me, for about two years ago I discovered them one day deep down in my memory, and I have known them ever since. He said:

'You are violent and uncivil, chamberlain. Why do you not let people go about their business?'

'Who is that?' interrupted my father with a cry.

'Someone who has every right to be here. She is no intruder. Christine Brahe.'

And again there was that same curiously attenuated silence, and once more the glass began to tremble. But my father broke abruptly away and rushed from the room.

I heard him pacing to and fro in his chamber all night long, for I, too, was unable to sleep. But suddenly, towards morning, I did wake out of a sort of drowsiness, and with a terror that paralysed me to the very heart, I saw something white seated on my bed. Despair finally gave me strength to thrust my head under the covers; and there I burst into tears for fear and helplessness. Suddenly I felt something cool and bright above my weeping eyes; I closed them over the tears so as not to have to see anything. But the voice that now spoke quite near to me came upon my face with a tepid, sweetish breath, and I recognised it: it was the voice of Fräulein Mathilde. I was instantly soothed, and albeit I was now re-assured, I still continued to let myself be comforted. I felt, indeed, that this kindness was rather effeminate, but for all that I enjoyed it and felt that I somehow deserved it.

'Auntie,' I said at last, and I tried to re-assemble

my mother's features scattered over her indeterminate countenance, 'Auntie, who was the lady?'

'Ah!' answered Fräulein Brahe, with a sigh that seemed ludicrous to me, 'an unfortunate lady, my child, an unfortunate lady.'

That same morning I noticed in one of the rooms several servants busy packing. I thought we were going to leave; it seemed to me quite natural that we should do so. Perhaps that was also my father's intention. I never learned what induced him to remain at Urne-kloster after that evening. But we did not leave. We stayed in that house eight or nine weeks longer, we endured the oppression of its peculiarities, and we saw Christine Brahe three times more.

At that time I knew nothing of her story. I did not know that she had died a long, long time before, at the birth of her second child, a boy who grew up to a fearful and cruel fate: I did not know that she was a dead woman. But my father knew it. Had he sought to force himself, uniting as he did a passionate temper with a clear and logical mind, calmly and without question to endure this adventure? I saw, without comprehending, how he struggled with himself; I felt, without understanding, how he finally mastered himself.

That was on the evening when we saw Christine Brahe for the last time. On this occasion Fräulein Mathilde had also appeared at dinner; but she was in an unusual mood. As in the first days after our arrival, she talked incessantly with no definite connection and in continual confusion, while some physical restlessness compelled her constantly to adjust something about her hair or her dress — until she suddenly jumped up with a shrill wailing cry and disappeared.

At the same moment my glance turned involuntarily to that particular door, and, in fact, Christine Brahe entered. My neighbour, the major, made a short, violent movement that was transmitted to my body, but evidently he no longer had the strength to rise. His brown, old, spotted visage turned from one to another, his mouth hung open and his tongue writhed behind his decayed teeth; then all at once his face had disappeared and his grey head lay on the table, his arms flung over it and under it as though they had been broken, and from somewhere a withered, speckled hand emerged and trembled.

And then Christine Brahe passed slowly through the room, like a sick person, step by step, in indescribable silence, broken only by a single whining sound like the whimper of an old dog. Then on the left of the huge silver swan filled with narcissi, the old man's great mask with its grey smile was thrust forward. He raised his wine-glass to my father. And then I saw how my father, just as Christine Brahe passed behind his chair, seized his glass and lifted it, as though it were a very heavy thing, a handsbreadth above the table.

And that same night we left Urnekloster.

*

HERE I sit, reading a poet. There are quite a number of people in the reading-room; but one is not aware of them. They are inside the books. They move, sometimes, within the pages like sleepers turning over between two dreams. Ah, how good it is to be among people who are reading! Why are they not always like that? You can go up to one of them and touch him lightly; he feels nothing. And if in rising, you chance to bump lightly against the person sitting next you and excuse yourself, he nods in the direction from which your voice comes, looking at you, but not seeing you; and his hair is like that of a man who has been asleep. How pleasant that is! And I sit here, and have a poet. What a fortunate lot is mine! There are perhaps three hundred people here just now, all reading; but it is impossible that each single one of them should have a poet. (Heaven knows what they have!) There are not three hundred poets. But consider what destiny has done for me, the shabbiest, perhaps, of all these readers, and a foreigner: I have a poet! Although I am poor. Although the suit I wear every day is beginning to show certain patches, and my shoes in some respects are not above reproach. True, my collar is clean, and my linen too, and I could, just as I am, enter any of the restaurants on the Grand Boulevards and reach confidently towards a plate of cakes and help myself. No one would be surprised; nor would they reprimand me and show me out; for my hand is still one that belongs in respectable society, a hand that is washed

four or five times a day. There is nothing under the
nails, the forefinger has no ink-stains, and the wrists,
particularly, are irreproachable. The poor never wash
so far up; that is a well-known fact. Certain conclu-
sions may therefore be drawn from the cleanness of
these wrists. And they are drawn. They are drawn in
the shops. But still there are one or two individuals, in
the Boulevard Saint-Michel, for example, and in the
rue Racine, who are not deceived. They refuse to take
my wrists seriously. They look at me and they know.
They know that I am really one of themselves, and
am only playing a little comedy. It is carnival-time,
you see. And they don't want to spoil my fun; they
just grin a little and wink at me. Not a soul has seen
them do this. Besides they treat me as though I were
a gentleman. If someone happens to be near, they
even become servile: they behave as if I had a fur
coat on and my carriage coming along behind me.
Sometimes I give them two sous, trembling lest they
should refuse them; but they take them. And all would
be well, had they not again grinned and winked at
me a little. Who are these people? What do they want
of me? Do they wait for me? How do they recognise
me? True, my beard looks somewhat neglected, and
very, very slightly resembles their own sickly, aged,
bleached beards, that have always impressed me. But
have I not the right to neglect my beard? Many busy
men do that, and it never occurs to anyone to reckon
them on that account among the social outcasts. For
it is clear to me that these people are the refuse of
society, and not simply mendicants. No, they are really

not mendicants; distinctions should be made. They are trash, the husks of humanity that fate has spewed out. Moist with the spittle of destiny they stick to a wall, a lamp-post, an advertisement-pillar, or they trickle slowly down a narrow alley, leaving a dark, dirty track behind them. What in the world did that old woman want with me, who had crawled out of some hole, carrying the drawer of a night-stand with a few buttons and needles rolling about in it? Why did she always walk beside me and watch me? As if she were trying to recognise me with her bleared eyes, that looked as though some diseased person had spat green slime under the bloody eyelids? And how came that little grey woman to stand once for a whole quarter of an hour by my side before a shop-window, showing me an old, long pencil, that was thrust with infinite slowness from her villainous, clenched hands? I pretended to look at the articles displayed in the window and not to notice anything. But she knew that I had seen her, she knew that I stood there wondering what she was really doing. For I understood quite well that the pencil in itself was of no consequence: I felt that it was a sign, a sign for the initiated, a sign that the outcasts know. I guessed she was indicating to me that I should go somewhere or do something. And the strangest thing about the whole affair was that I could not rid myself of the feeling that there actually existed a certain compact to which this sign belonged, and that this scene was in truth something that I should have expected.

That was two weeks ago. But scarcely a day passes

now without a similar encounter. Not only in the twilight, but at midday in the most frequented streets, a little man or an old woman will suddenly appear, nod to me, show me something, and then vanish, as though everything necessary were now done. It is possible that one day it may occur to them to come as far as my room. They certainly know where I live, and they will take care that the concierge does not stop them. But here in the library, my dears, here I am safe from you. One must have a special card in order to get into this room. In possessing that card I have the advantage over you. I go a little shyly, as one may well imagine, through the streets; but finally I stand before a glass door, open it as if I were at home, show my card at the next door (just exactly as you show me your things, only with the difference that people understand me, and know what I mean —), and then I am among these books, am withdrawn from you as though I were dead, and sit and read a poet.

You do not know what a poet is? Verlaine... You know nothing about him? Have no recollection of him? No. You did not distinguish him from among those whom you knew? You make no distinctions, I know. But it is another poet I am reading, quite another, one who does not live in Paris; one who has a quiet home in the mountains. He rings like a bell in clear air. A happy poet who tells of his window and the glass doors of his book-case, that pensively reflect a favourite, lonely view. This poet it is that I should have liked to become; for he knows so many things about young girls, and I, too, should have known a great deal about them. He knows about young girls who lived a hundred years ago; it matters no more that they are dead, for he knows everything. And that is the main thing. He reads their names aloud — those slight, elegantly-written names with old-fashioned loops in their capital letters, and the grown-up names of their older girl-friends, in the sound of which just the least accent of fate is mingled, just the least hint of disillusion and death. Perhaps their faded letters, the loose leaves of their diaries recording birthdays, summer parties, then birthdays again, are lying in a compartment of his mahogany desk. Or mayhap there is a drawer in some capacious wardrobe at the back of his bedroom, in which their spring garments are kept — white dresses worn for the first time at Easter, dresses of flowered tulle which properly belong to summer but for which they could not wait. Oh, what a happy fate, to sit in the quiet room of an ancestral house, surrounded by calm, sedentary things, and to hear the first tomtits trying their skill outside in the sunny, light-green garden, and in the distance the village clock! To sit and watch a warm streak of afternoon sun, and to know many things about girls of bygone days, and to be a poet. And to think that I, too, might have become such a poet, had I been allowed to dwell anywhere, anywhere in the world, say, in one of the many closed-up country houses about which no one troubles any more. I would have required only one room — the sunny room in the gable end. I would have lived there with my ancient possessions, my family portraits, and my books. An arm-chair I would have had and flowers and dogs, and a stout stick for the stony roads. And nothing more. Only a book bound in yellowish, ivory-coloured leather, with an antique design of flowers on its fly-leaf: in that book I would have written. I would have written a great deal, for I would have had many thoughts and memories of many people.

But things have fallen out otherwise, God knows why. My old furniture is rotting in a barn where I have been allowed to put it, while I myself — yes, my God! — have no roof over me, and the rain is driving into my eyes.

*

OCCASIONALLY I pass by little shops — in the rue de Seine, for example. They are the shops of antiquaries and of petty dealers in old books or engravings, with overcrowded windows. No one ever enters them; their owners apparently do no business. But if you glance in, you can see them sitting there, sitting and reading, without a care; they take no thought for the morrow, they are not anxious to succeed; a dog lies good-naturedly at their feet, or a cat makes the stillness greater by gliding along the rows of books, as if it were rubbing the names off their bindings.

Ah, if that were enough! I have often wished to buy such an overcrowded shop-window for myself and to sit behind it with my dog for twenty years.

*

It is good to say it out aloud: 'Nothing has happened.' Once again: 'Nothing has happened.' Does that help?

That my stove began to smoke again and I had to go out, was really no misfortune. It is of no consequence whatever that I feel chilled and weary. If I have been running about the narrow streets all day, it is my own fault. I might just as well have sat in the Louvre. But, no, I could not have done that. There are certain people who go there to warm themselves. They sit on the velvet-covered benches and their feet stand side by side like big empty boots on the gratings of the hot-air registers. They are very modest, and they are thankful when the attendants in their dark-blue uniforms studded with medals suffer their presence. But when I enter, they make faces. They grimace and slightly nod. And then, when I move about looking at the pictures, they keep me in view, always in view, always within reach of their confluent, lack-lustre gaze. So it was just as well I did not go to the Louvre. I have been walking incessantly. Heaven knows through how many towns, districts, cemeteries, bridges, and lanes. Somewhere or other I saw a man pushing a barrow with vegetables. He was shouting, *'Chou-fleur, chou-fleur,'* pronouncing the 'fleur' with a strangely muffled 'eu.' An angular, ugly woman walked beside him, nudging him from time to time, and when she nudged him, he shouted. Sometimes he shouted of his own accord, but then his shout was useless, and he had to shout again immediately after because they were in front of a customer's house. Have I already said that the man was blind? No? Well, he was blind. He was blind and he shouted. No, I falsify when I say only that; I am suppressing the barrow he was shoving; I am pretending I did not notice he was shouting 'cauliflower.' But is that essential? Even if it were, does that not depend on what the whole thing meant for me? I saw an old man who was blind and shouted. That I saw. Saw.

Will anyone believe that such houses exist? No, they will say again that I am falsifying. But this time it is the truth, nothing omitted, and naturally nothing added. Where should I get it from? Everyone knows that I am poor. Everyone knows that. Houses? But, to be precise, they were houses that were no longer there. Houses that had been demolished from top to bottom. It was the other houses that were there, those that had stood alongside of them, tall neighbouring houses. Apparently these were in danger of falling down, since they had been deprived of all support from the adjoining structures; for a whole scaffolding of long, tarred poles had been rammed slantwise between the rubbish-strewn ground and the exposed wall. I do not know whether I have already said that it is this wall I mean. But it was, so to speak, not the first wall of the existing houses (as one would have supposed), but the last wall of the houses that were there no longer. One saw its inner side. One saw, at the different storeys, the walls of the rooms to which the paper still clung, and here and there marks of the beams of flooring or ceiling. Near the bedroom partitions there still remained, along the whole length of the wall, a greyish-white streak; across this there crept in worm-like spirals that seemed to serve some unspeakably disgusting digestive function, the gaping, rust-covered channel of the water-closet pipe. At the ceiling edges remained grey, dusty traces of the paths the gas-pipes had followed; they bent hither and thither, taking unexpected turns, and ran along the painted walls into a black hole that had been carelessly torn out. But the walls themselves were the most unforgettable. The stubborn life of these rooms had not allowed itself to be trampled out. It was still there; it clung to the nails that had been left in the walls; it found a resting-place on the remaining handsbreadth of flooring; it squatted beneath the corner beams where a little bit of space remained. One could see it in the colours which it had slowly changed, year by year: blue into a mouldy green, green into grey, and yellow into a stale, drab, weary white. But it was also in the places that had kept fresher, behind the mirrors, the pictures, and the wardrobes; for it had outlined their contours over and over again, and had been with cobwebs and dust even in these hidden retreats that now lay uncovered. It was in every bare, flayed streak of surface, it was in the blisters the dampness had raised at the edges of the wallpapers; it floated in the torn-off shreds, and sweated out of the long-standing spots of filth. And from these walls once blue, and green and yellow, framed by the tracks of the disturbed partitions, the breath of these lives came forth —the clammy, sluggish, fusty breath, which no wind had yet scattered. There were the midday meals and

the sicknesses and the exhalations and the smoke of
years, and the sweat that breaks out under the arm-
pits and makes the garments heavy, and the stale
breath of mouths, and the oily odour of perspiring feet.
There were the pungent tang of urine and the stench
of burning soot and the grey reek of potatoes, and the
heavy, sickly fumes of rancid grease. The sweetish,
lingering smell of neglected infants was there, and the
smell of frightened children who go to school, and the
stuffiness of the beds of nubile youths. To these was
added much that had risen from the pit of the reeking
street below, and more that had oozed down from
above with the rain, which over cities is not clean.
And much the feeble, tamed, domestic winds, that
always stay in the same street, had borne thither; and
much more was there, the sources of which were not
known. I said, did I not, that all the walls had been
demolished except the last — ? It is of this wall I have
been speaking all along. One would think that I had
stood a long time before it; but I can swear that I
began to run as soon as I had recognised it. For that
is the terrible thing, that I did recognise it. I recognise
everything here, and that is why it takes immediate
possession of me: it is quite at home in me.

After these experiences I was somewhat worn out,
I might even say exhausted, and that is why it was
too much for me that he, too, should still have been
awaiting me. He waited in the little dairy shop where
I intended to eat two poached eggs. I was hungry; I
had not touched food the whole day. But even then
I could not eat anything; before the eggs were ready I

was driven out again into the streets, that rushed towards me in a viscid flood of humanity. For it was carnival, and evening, and the people had abundant leisure and roved about, jostling one another. Their faces shone in the flares of the show-booths, and the laughter bubbled from their mouths like matter from open sores. The more impatiently I tried to force my way forwards, the more they laughed, and the more closely they crowded together. Somehow a woman's shawl hooked itself to me; I dragged her after me, and people stopped me and laughed, and I felt that I should laugh too, but I could not. Someone threw a handful of confetti into my eyes, and it stung like a whip. At the street-crossings people were closely wedged together, shoved one into the other, and there was no forward movement in them, only a quiet, gentle swaying back and forth, as though they standing paired themselves. But although they were stationary, and I was running like a madman along the edge of the pavement, where there were gaps in the crowd, the truth was that it was they who were moving while I never stirred. For nothing changed; when I looked up I was still aware of the same houses on the one side and on the other the booths. Perhaps everything was indeed standing still, and it was simply a dizziness in me and in them, which seemed to whirl everything around. I had no time to reflect on this; I was heavy with sweat, and a stupefying pain was circling in me, as if something too large were being driven with my blood, which distended the veins, wherever it passed. And withal I felt that the air had long been exhausted, and that I was now breathing only exhalations, which my lungs rejected.

But it is over now; I have survived it. I am sitting in my room near the lamp; it is a little cold, for I do not venture to try the stove: what if it were to smoke, and I should have to go out again? I am sitting and thinking: if I were not so poor I should rent another room with furniture not quite so worn, not quite so reminiscent of former occupants, as the furniture here. At first it really cost me an effort to lean my head on this arm-chair; for there is, in its green covering, a greasy, grey hollow, into which all heads seem to fit. For a long time I took the precaution of putting a handkerchief under my hair, but now I am too tired to do that; I discovered that it is well as it is, and that the slight cavity is made exactly for the back of my head, as if to measure. But if I were not poor, I should first of all buy a good stove, and burn the clean, strong wood that comes from the mountains, and not this comfortless *tête de moineau,* the fumes of which make breathing so timid and the brain so confused. And then I should need someone to come and tidy up without making coarse noises, and to keep the fire just as I like it. For often when I have to kneel before the stove and poke for a quarter of an hour, the skin on my forehead tense with the close glow and with heat in my open eyes, I exhaust all the strength I have in reserve for the day, and when I go among people afterwards, they naturally get the better of me very easily. I should sometimes, when the crush is great, take a carriage, and drive by; I should dine every day at a Duval. . . . I should no longer slink into cream-eries. . . . Would he, too, have been in a Duval? No. He would never have been allowed to wait for me there. They do not allow dying people to enter such places. Dying people? I am now sitting in my room; so I can try to reflect quietly on what happened to me. It is well to leave nothing uncertain. I went in, then, and at first only noticed that the table at which I usually sat was occupied by someone else. I bowed in the direction of the little counter, gave my order, and sat down at a table near by. But then I felt him, although he did not stir. It was precisely this immobility of his that I felt, and I understood it all at once. The connection between us was established, and I knew that he had become stiff with terror. I knew that the terror had paralysed him, terror at something that was happening within himself. Perhaps one of his blood-vessels had burst; perhaps, just at this moment, some poison that he had long dreaded had penetrated a ventricle of his heart; perhaps a huge abscess had risen in his brain like a sun, changing the world for him. With an in-describable effort I compelled myself to look in his direction; for I still hoped it was all imagination. But in the end I sprang up and rushed out of the place; for I had made no mistake. He sat there in a thick, dark, winter cloak, and his grey, strained face was buried deep in a woollen neckcloth. His mouth was closed as if a heavy weight rested on it; but it was not possible to say if his eyes still saw anything; they were hidden by moist, smoke-grey glasses, which trembled slightly. His nostrils were distended, and the long hair on his wasted temples wilted as if in too intense a heat. His ears were long, yellow, with large shadows behind them. Yes, he knew that at that moment he was withdrawing from everything, not merely from human beings. A moment more and everything will have lost its meaning, and that table and the cup, and the chair to which he clings, all the near and commonplace things around him, will have become unintelligible, strange and burdensome. So he sat there and waited until it should have happened. And defended himself no longer.

And I still defend myself. I defend myself, although I know that my heart has been torn out, and that even if my tormentors left me alone, I could no longer live. I say to myself: 'Nothing has happened,' and yet I was only able to understand that man because something is happening within me too, that is beginning to draw me away and separate me from everything. How it always horrified me to hear it said of a dying person that he could no longer recognise anybody! Then I would imagine to myself a lonely face that raised itself from pillows and sought, sought for some familiar thing, sought for something once seen, but there was nothing there. If my fear were not so great, I should console myself with the fact that it is not impossible to see things in a different way and yet to live. But I am afraid; I am filled with a nameless fear at this change. I am, indeed, not yet accustomed to this world, which seems good to me. What should I do in another? I should so gladly stay among the significances that have become dear to me; and if something must already change, I should like at least to be allowed to live among dogs, who possess a world akin to our own and the same things.

For a while yet I can write all this down and say it. But there will come a day when my hand will be distant from me, and when I bid it write, it will write words I do not mean. The day of that other interpretation will dawn, when no word will properly follow another, and all meanings will dissolve like clouds, and fall down like rain. Despite my fear I am yet like one standing in the presence of great things; and I remember that I used often to feel like this when I was about to write. But this time I shall be written. I am the impression that will transform itself. Ah! but a little more, and I could understand all this and approve it. Only a step, and my deep woe would be beatitude! But I cannot take that step; I have fallen and can rise no more, for I am broken. I have always believed that some help might come. There it lies before me in my own handwriting, what I have prayed, evening after evening. I transcribed it from the books in which I found it, so that it might be very near me, issued from my hand like something of my own. And now I want to write it once again, here on my knees before my table I want to write it; for thus I have it longer than when I read it, and every word endures, and has time to die away.

'Mécontent de tous et mécontent de moi, je voudrais bien me racheter et m'enorgueillir un peu dans

*le silence et la solitude de la nuit. Âmes de ceux que
j'ai aimés, âmes de ceux que j'ai chantés, fortifiez-moi,
soutenez-moi, éloignez de moi le mensonge et les
vapeurs corruptrices du monde; et vous, Seigneur mon
Dieu! accordez-moi la grâce de produire quelques
beaux vers qui me prouvent à moi-meme que je ne suis
pas le dernier des hommes, que je ne suis pas inférieur
à ceux que je méprise.'* *

'They were children of fools, yea, children of base
men: they were viler than the earth.

And now I am their song, yea, I am their byword.
... They raise up against me the ways of their destruc-
tion.

They mar my path, they set forward my calamity,
they have no helper....

And now my soul is poured out upon me; the
days of affliction have taken hold upon me.

My bones are pierced in me in the night seasons:
and my sinews take no rest.

By the great force of my disease is my garment
changed: it bindeth me about as the collar of my
coat....

My bowels boiled and rested not: the days of afflic-
tion prevented me....

---

* Dissatisfied with everyone, and dissatisfied with myself, I
earnestly desire to redeem myself and take a little pride in myself,
in the silence and solitude of the night. Souls of those whom I have
loved, souls of those whom I have sung, strengthen me, support me,
keep far from me the falsehood and the corrupting vapours of the
world; and Thou, O Lord my God! grant me the grace to produce
some noble verse, that shall be proof to myself that I am not the
least of men, that I am not lower than those whom I despise.

My harp also is turned to mourning, and my organ into the voice of them that weep.'

*

THE doctor did not understand me. Not at all. And certainly my case was difficult to describe. He wanted to try electric treatment. Good. I received a printed form: I had to be at the Salpetrière at one o'clock. I was there. I had to pass a long row of barracks and traverse a number of courtyards, where people, in white bonnets that made them look like convicts, stood here and there under the bare trees. At length I entered a long, gloomy, corridor-like room, that had on one side four windows of dim, greenish glass, separated from one another by a broad stretch of black wall. A wooden bench ran along its whole length, and on this bench they who knew me sat, and waited. Yes, they were all there. When I became accustomed to the twilight of the place, I noticed that among them, as they sat shoulder to shoulder in an interminable row, there were also other people, insignificant people, artisans, servants, carters. Beyond, at the narrow far end of this corridor, two stout women had spread themselves out on chairs, and were conversing; concierges probably. I looked at the clock; it was five minutes to one. In five minutes, or say ten, my turn would come; so it was not so bad. The air was vile, heavy, impregnated with clothes and breaths. At one point, the strong cool smell of ether came through a partly opened door. I began to walk up and down. It crossed my mind that I had been directed here, among these people, to this overcrowded, public consultation. It was, so to speak, the first official confirmation of the fact that I belonged among the outcasts; had the doctor known by my appearance? Yet I had paid my visit in tolerably decent garments; I had sent in my card. Despite that he must have learned it somehow; perhaps I had betrayed myself. However, now that it was a fact I did not find it so bad after all. The people sat quietly and took no notice of me. Some were in pain and swung one leg a little in order to endure it better. Several of the men had laid their heads in the palms of their hands; others were slumbering deeply, with heavy, distorted faces. A stout man with a red, swollen neck sat bending forward, staring at the floor, and spitting from time to time with a smack at a spot he seemed to find suitable for the purpose. A child was sobbing in a corner; it had drawn up its long thin legs beneath it on the bench, and now clasped and held them tightly to its body, as though it must bid them farewell. A small, pale woman on whose head a crape hat adorned with round, black flowers, sat awry, wore the grimace of a smile on her pitiable lips, but her sore eyes were constantly overflowing. Not far from her had been placed a girl with a round, smooth face, and protruding eyes that were without expression; her mouth hung open, so that one saw her white, slimy gums with their old, decayed teeth. And there were many bandages. Bandages that swathed a whole head layer upon layer, until only a single eye remained that no longer belonged to anyone. Bandages that hid, and bandages that revealed, what was beneath them. Bandages that had been undone, in which, as in a dirty bed, a hand now lay that was a hand no longer; and a bandaged leg that protruded from the row on the bench, as large as a whole man. I walked up and down, and endeavoured to be calm. I occupied myself a good deal with the wall facing me. I noticed that it contained a number of single doors, and was not carried up to the ceiling, so that this corridor was not completely separated from the rooms that must adjoin it. I looked at the clock; I had been pacing up and down for an hour. A little later the doctors arrived. First a couple of young fellows who passed by with indifferent faces, and finally the one I had consulted, in light gloves, *chapeau à huit reflets,* impeccable overcoat. When he saw me he lifted his hat a little and smiled absent-mindedly. I now hoped to be called immediately, but another hour passed. I cannot remember how I spent it. It passed. An old man wearing a soiled apron, a sort of attendant, came and touched me on the shoulder. I entered one of the adjoining rooms. The doctor and the youths sat round a table and looked at me. Someone gave me a chair. So far so good. And now I had to describe what it was that was the matter with me. As briefly as possible, *s'il vous plaît.* For much time these gentlemen had not. I felt singularly uncomfortable. The young fellows sat and examined me with that superior, professional curiosity which they had learned. The doctor I knew stroked his black, pointed beard and smiled absently. I thought I should burst into tears, but I heard myself saying in fluent French: 'I have already had the honour, monsieur, of giving you all the details that I can give. If you consider it indispensable that these gentlemen should be initiated, then you are certainly able, from the conversation we had, to tell them in a few words, while I find it extremely painful to do so.' The doctor rose, smiling politely, and going towards the window with his assistants said a few words, which he accompanied with a vague, horizontal movement of his hands. Three minutes later one of the young men, short-sighted and impetuous, came back to the table, and said, trying to look at me severely, 'Do you sleep well, sir?' 'No, badly.' Whereupon he rushed back again to the group at the window. There they discussed my case a little longer, then the doctor turned to me and informed me that I would be summoned again. I reminded him that my appointment had been for one o'clock. He smiled and made a few swift, abrupt movements with his small white hands, which were meant to signify that he was uncommonly busy. So I returned to my lobby, where the air had become much more oppressive, and began again to pace up and down, although I felt mortally tired. Finally the humid, accumulated smell made me dizzy; I stopped at the entrance door and opened it a little. I saw that outside it was still afternoon and still sunny, and that did me ever so much good. But I had hardly stood there a minute when I heard someone calling me. A female sitting at a table two or three steps away lisped something to me. Who had told me to open the door? I said I could not stand the atmosphere of the room.

Well, that was my own affair, but the door had to be kept shut. Was it not permissible, then, to open a window? No, that was forbidden. I decided to resume my walking up and down; for after all that was a kind of anodyne, and it hurt nobody. But now this too displeased the woman sitting at the little table. Did I not have a seat? No, I hadn't. Walking about was not allowed; I would have to find a seat. There ought to be one vacant. The woman was right. In fact, a place was promptly found next the girl with the protruding eyes. There I now sat with the sense that this situation must certainly portend something dreadful. On my left, then, was this girl with the rotting gums; what was on my right I could not make out till after some time. It was a huge, immovable mass, that had a face and a large, heavy, inert hand. The side of the face that I saw was empty, quite without features and without memories; and it was gruesome that its attire was like that of a corpse dressed for the coffin. The narrow, black cravat had been tied in the same loose, impersonal way around the collar, and it was evident that the coat had been put on the will-less body by other hands. The hand had been placed on the trousers exactly where it lay, and even the hair looked as if it had been combed by those women who lay out the dead, and stuck up stiffly like the fur of stuffed animals. I observed all these things with close attention, and it occurred to me that this must be the place that had been destined for me; for I now at last believed that I had arrived at that stage of my life at which I should remain. Yes, fate goes wonderful ways.

Suddenly there burst out not far from me, in quick succession, the cries of a terrified, struggling child, followed by a low, suppressed weeping. While I was straining to discover where this noise could have come from, a faint, choked cry quavered again, and I heard voices, questioning, and the voice of someone giving orders in a subdued tone; after that, some sort of machine began to hum, buzzing indifferently away. Then I recalled that half wall, and I realised that all these noises came from the other side of the doors, and that work was going on in there. Indeed, the attendant with the soiled apron appeared from time to time and made a sign. I had given up thinking that he might mean me. Was it intended for me this time? No. Two men appeared with a wheeled arm-chair. They lifted the mass beside me into it, and I now saw that it was an old, paralysed man, who had another side to him, a smaller side worn out by life, and an open, troubled, melancholy eye. They took him inside, and now there was plenty of room beside me. And I sat and wondered what they were likely to do to the imbecile girl and whether she, too, would scream. Behind the wall the machines whirred pleasantly like machines in a factory; there was nothing disturbing about it.

But suddenly everything was quiet, and in the silence, a pretentious, self-complacent voice, which I thought I knew, said: *'Riez!'* A pause. *'Riez! Mais riez, riez!'* I was already laughing myself. It was inexplicable that the man on the other side of the partition was not willing to laugh. A machine rattled, but immediately became quiet again. Words were exchanged, then the same energetic voice rose again, and ordered: *'Dites-nous le mot: avant.'* And spelling it: *'A-v-a-n-t.'* Silence. *'On n'intend rien. Encore une fois ...'*

And then, as I listened to the hot, flaccid stuttering on the other side of the partition, then for the first time in many, many years it was there, the Big Thing that had filled me with my first, profound fear, when as a child I lay ill with fever. Yes, that was what I had always called it, when they all stood around my bed, and felt my pulse, and asked me what had frightened me: the Big Thing. And when they sent for the doctor, and he came and spoke to me, I begged him only to get the Big Thing to go away, nothing else mattered. But he was like the rest. He could not take it away, albeit I was so small then and might so easily have been helped. And now it was there again. Later it had simply stayed away; it had not even come on the nights when I had fever; but now it was there, although I had no fever. Now it was there. Now it grew out of me like a tumour, like a second head; it seemed to be part of myself, yet it surely could not belong to me, since it was so large. It was there like a huge, dead beast, that had once, when it was still alive, been my hand or my arm. And my blood flowed both through me and through it, as if through one and the same body. And my heart had to make a painful effort to drive the blood into it; there was hardly enough blood there. And the blood went into it unwillingly, and came back sickly and tainted. But the Big Thing gathered and grew before my face, like a warm, bluish boil; it extended beyond my mouth, and already the shadow of its edge lay over my remaining eye.

I cannot recall how I got back through the numerous courtyards. It was evening, and I was lost in this strange neighbourhood and went up boulevards with interminable walls in one direction, and when there was no end to them, returned in the opposite direction until I reached some square or other. Then I began to walk along a street, and other streets appeared that I had never seen before, and still more streets. Electric cars, too brilliantly lit, ran furiously up and past with their harsh clang of bells. But on their signboards stood names that I did not know. I did not know in what city I was, or whether I had a lodging anywhere, or what I ought to do in order not to have to go on walking.

*

AND now this malady, which has always affected me so strangely. I am sure its importance is minimised, just as the importance of other diseases is exaggerated. This disease has no particular characteristics; it takes on those of the person it attacks. With a somnambulic assurance it drags from the profoundest depths of each one's being a danger that seemed passed, and sets it before him again, quite near, imminent. Men, who once in their school-days attempted the helpless vice that has for its duped partner the poor, hard hands of boys, find themselves tempted afresh by it; or an illness they had conquered in childhood recurs in them; or a lost habit re-appears, a certain hesitating turn of the head that had been peculiar to them years before. And with whatever comes, there rises a whole medley of confused memories, which hangs about it like wet seaweed on something long sunk in the sea. Lives of which one never knew mount to the surface and mingle with what has actually been, and obliterate past things that one had thought to know: for in that which ascends is a fresh, rested strength, but that which has always been there is wearied by too much remembrance.

I am lying in my bed five flights up, and my day, which nothing interrupts, is like a clock-face without hands. As a thing long lost lies one morning in its old place, uninjured and whole, fresher almost than on the day of its disappearance, quite as though someone had been taking care of it — so here and there on my coverlet lie lost things out of my childhood, and are as new. All forgotten fears are there again.

The fear that a small, woollen thread that sticks out of the hem of my blanket may be hard, hard and sharp like a steel needle; the fear that this little button on my night-shirt may be bigger than my head, large and heavy; the fear that this crumb of bread that is falling from my bed may be shattered like glass when it reaches the floor, and the oppressive anxiety lest therewith everything break to pieces, everything for ever; the fear that the torn scrap of an opened letter may be something forbidden that no one ought to see, something indescribably precious for which no place in the room is secure enough; the fear that if I fell asleep I might swallow the piece of coal lying in front of the stove; the fear that some numeral may begin to grow in my brain until there is no more room for it within me; the fear that it may be granite I am lying on, grey granite; the fear that I may shout, and that people may gather at my door and finally break it open; the fear that I may betray myself and tell all that I dread; and the fear that I might not be able to say anything, because everything is beyond utterance; and the other fears ... the fears.

I prayed for my childhood and it has come back to me, and I feel that it is just as burdensome as it was before, and that I have grown older to no purpose.

*

YESTERDAY my fever was better, and this morning the day began like a day in spring, the spring in pictures. I will try to go out and visit my poet in the Bibliothèque Nationale, whom I have left so long unread, and perhaps later I can walk quietly through the gardens. Perhaps there will be wind on the big pond which has such real water, and children will come to launch their boats with the red sails and watch them.

Today I really did not expect it; I went out so bravely, doing, as I thought, the simplest and most natural thing in the world. And yet, something came again, which took me like paper, crumpled me up and threw me away; something unprecedented.

The Boulevard Saint-Michel lay deserted and vast, and it was easy to walk along its gentle incline. Window-casements opened overhead with a glassy ring, and the flash of them flew across the street like a white bird. A carriage with vivid red wheels rolled past, and further down someone was carrying something bright green. Horses in gleaming harness trotted on the dark, freshly-sprinkled carriage-way. The wind was brisk, fresh, mild, and everything rose on the air: odours, cries, bells.

I passed in front of one of those cafés where sham gypsies in red jackets usually play of an evening. From the open windows the air of the past night crept out with a bad conscience. Sleek-haired waiters were busy sweeping in front of the door. One of them was bending over, throwing handful after handful of yellow sand under the tables. A passer-by nudged him and pointed down the boulevard. The waiter, who was all red in the face, looked sharply for a little in that direction, and then a laugh spread over his beardless cheeks, as thought it had been spilled across them. He beckoned to the other waiters, and laughing all the while, turned his head rapidly several times, right and left, so as to draw the attention of all, while missing nothing of the scene himself. Now they all stood gazing or searching down the street, smiling or annoyed that they had not yet discovered what was so amusing.

I felt the twinge of an incipient fear. Something urged me over to the other side of the street; but I only began to walk faster and glanced involuntarily at the few people in front of me, about whom I noticed nothing unusual. Still I saw that one of them, an errand-boy with a blue apron and an empty basket on his shoulder, was staring after someone. When he had had enough, he wheeled round where he stood towards the houses and signalled across the street to a laughing clerk with that waving gesture of the hand before the forehead which is familiar to everyone. Then his dark eyes flashed and he came towards me swaggering and content.

I expected, as soon as I could get a better view, to see some unusual and striking figure; but apparently there was no one in front of me save a tall, emaciated man in a dark overcoat and with a soft black hat on his short, faded, blonde hair. I made sure there was nothing laughable about this man's clothing or behaviour, and I was already trying to look beyond him down the boulevard, when he stumbled over something. As I was following close behind him I was on my guard, but when I came to the place there was nothing there, absolutely nothing. We both walked on, he and I, the distance between us remaining the same. Then there came a street-crossing, and there the man ahead of me hopped down from the pavement to the street, one foot held high, somewhat as children walking now and again hop and skip, when they are happy. On the other side of the crossing, he simply made one long step up. But no sooner was he up than he raised one leg a little, and jumped high into the air with the other, immediately repeating this action again and again. One might easily have taken this abrupt movement for a stumble, had one persuaded oneself that some small object, a pip, a slippery fruit-peel, or something of the sort had lain on the pavement; and the strange thing was that the man himself appeared to believe in the presence of an obstacle; for he turned round every time and looked at the offending spot with that half-annoyed, half-reproachful air people have at such moments. Once again something warned me to take the other side of the street, but I did not obey; I continued to follow this man, riveting my whole attention on his legs. I must admit that I felt considerably relieved when for about twenty steps this hopping did not recur; but as I raised my eyes I noticed that something else had begun to trouble the man. The collar of his overcoat had got thrust up, and try as he would to put it down again, now with one hand, now with both at once, he did not succeed. Things like that might happen to anyone; I was in no way disquieted. But then I perceived with the liveliest astonishment that in the man's busy hands there were two movements: one a rapid, secret movement, that covertly lifted the collar up, and the other, elaborate, prolonged, as if spelled out with exaggerated slowness, that was meant to put it down. This observation disconcerted me so very much that two minutes passed before I realised that the same horrible, two-beat hopping movement which had just left the man's legs was now in his neck, behind the thrust-up collar of his overcoat and his nervously agitated hands. From that moment I was bound to him. I saw that this hopping impulse was wandering about his body, trying to break out at different points. I understood why he was afraid of people, and I myself began to examine the passers-by cautiously to see if they noticed anything. A cold stab went through me when his legs suddenly made a slight, jerking spring; but no one saw it, and I thought to myself that I would also stumble a little in case anyone began to notice. That would certainly be one way of making the curious believe that there had really been some trifling, unapparent obstacle in the road, on which both of us had happened to tread. But, while I was thus considering how I might help him, he had himself discovered a new and excellent expedient. I forgot to mention that he carried a stick; it was an ordinary stick, made of dark wood with a smooth, curved handle. In his anxious search for some plan, the idea had occurred to him of holding this stick against his back, at first with one of his hands (for who knew what the other might yet be needed for?) right along his spine, pressing it firmly into the small of his back, and thrusting the curved end under his coat-collar, so that it could be seen standing up like a supporting bar between his neck and the first dorsal vertebra. This attitude was by no means odd; at most it was the least bit insolent, but the unexpected spring day might excuse that. No one thought of turning round to look, and now all went well. Wonderfully well. It is true that at the next crossing two hops broke out, two little, half-suppressed hops, but they did not amount to anything; and the only really visible leap was so cleverly managed (a hose-pipe lay right across the street) that there was nothing to be afraid of. Yes, things were still going well. From time to time the other hand seized the stick and pressed it in more firmly, and at once the danger was again averted. Yet I could not keep my anxiety from growing. I knew that as he walked and made ceaseless efforts to appear indifferent and absent-minded, that awful convulsive motion was accumulating in his body; I, too, experienced the anxiety with which he felt it growing and growing, and I saw how he clung to his stick, when the jerking began within him. The expression of his hands then became so severe and unrelenting that I placed all my hope in his will, which was bound to be strong. But what could a will do here? The moment must come when the man's strength would be exhausted; it could not be long now. And I, walking behind him with quickly-beating heart, I gathered my little strength together like gold, and, gazing at his hands, I besought him to take it if he needed it.

I believe that he took it; how could I help the fact that it was not more?

At the Place Saint-Michel there were many vehicles and people hurrying hither and thither. We were several times held up between two carriages; he took breath then, and let himself go a little, by way of rest, and there would be a slight hopping and a little jerking of the head. Perhaps that was the ruse by which the imprisoned malady sought to get the better of him. His will had given way at two points, and the concession had left behind in the obsessed muscles a gentle, enticing stimulation and this compelling two-beat rhythm. But the stick was still in its place, and the hands looked sinister and wrathful. In this fashion we set foot on the bridge, and all was well — all was still well. But now his gait became noticeably uncertain; sometimes he ran a few steps, sometimes he stood. Stood. His left hand gently released the stick and rose, rose, so slowly that I saw it tremble in the air; he thrust his hat back a little, and drew his hand across his brow. He turned his head slightly, and his gaze wavered over sky, houses and water, without grasping anything. And then he gave in. His stick had gone, he stretched out his arms as if he meant to fly, and then something like a natural force broke out of him, bent him forward and dragged him back, kept him nodding and bowing, and flung him dancing into the midst of the crowd. For already there were many people round him, and I saw him no more.

What sense would there have been in my going any further? I was empty. Like a blank sheet of paper I drifted along past the houses up the boulevard again.

*

*I AM attempting to write to you, although there is really nothing to say after an enforced leave-taking. I am attempting it nevertheless; I think I must, because I have seen the saint in the Panthéon, the solitary, saintly woman, and the roof, and the door, and the lamp inside with its modest circle of light, and beyond the sleeping city and the river and the moon-lit distance. The saint watches over the sleeping city. I wept. I wept, because it was all so immediately and unex-

* A rough draft of a letter.

pectedly present. I wept as I looked; I could not help myself.

I am in Paris; those who learn this are glad, most of them envy me. They are right. It is a great city; great and full of strange temptations. For myself I must admit that I have in a certain measure succumbed to them. I think there is no other way of saying it. I have succumbed to these temptations, and this has caused certain modifications, if not in my character, at least in my outlook on the world, and, in any case, in my life itself. Under these influences I have begun to form an entirely different conception of everything; certain differences have appeared that separate me more than any of my previous experiences from other men. A world transformed. A new life filled with new meanings. For the moment I find it a little hard because everything is too new. I am a novice in dealing with the circumstances of my own life.

Would it not be possible for once to get a glimpse of the sea?

Yes, but only think, I imagined you might come. Could you perhaps have told me if there was a doctor? I forgot to ask about that. Besides, I no longer need the information.

Do you recollect Baudelaire's incredible poem, *'Une Charogne'*? Perhaps I understand it now. Except for the last verse he was within his rights. What else could he have done after such an experience? It was his business to see in those terrible things, repulsive in appearance only, that being which alone is of value in all that exists. There is no choice or refusal. Do you

68

imagine it was by chance that Flaubert wrote his *Saint Julien l'Hospitalier?* This, it seems to me, is the test: whether a man can bring himself to lie beside a leper and warm him with the glow of a lover's heart. From such a deed only good could result.

But do not imagine that I am suffering from disappointment here — quite the contrary. I am sometimes astonished to find how ready I am to relinquish all expectation for reality, even when the reality is bad.

My God, if any of it could be shared! But would it *exist* then, would it *exist?* No, it is possible only at the price of solitude.

*

THE existence of the horrible in every particle of air! You breathe it in as something transparent; but inside you it condenses, hardens, assumes pointed, geometrical forms between your organs. For all the torments and the agonies wrought on scaffolds, in torture-chambers, mad-houses, operating-theatres, under the vaults of bridges in late autumn: all these have a stubborn imperishability, all these persist and, jealous of all else that is, cling to their frightful reality. People would like to be allowed to forget many of these things; sleep softly files down the grooves they have made in their brains, but dreams drive sleep away and trace the furrows again. And then one wakes up panting and lets the gleam of a candle melt into the darkness, and drinks like sugared water the twilight quietude. But, alas, on how narrow a ledge this security rests! Only the slightest movement, and once again vision plunges beyond things known and friendly, and the contour but now so consoling, grows clearer as an outlined edge of terror. Beware of the light that makes space more hollow; look not around to see whether, perchance, behind you as you sit up, a shadow has arisen that will master you. Better perhaps to have remained in the darkness, and your unconfined heart would have sought to bear the whole indistinguishable burden. You have now pulled yourself together; you perceive the limits of your being within your own hands; you trace from time to time with an uncertain gesture the outline of your face. And there is scarcely any room within you; and it almost calms you to think that nothing very large can abide in this restricted space; that even the unheard-of must become an inward thing and must shrink to fit itself to its surroundings. But outside — outside there is no limit to it. And when the level outside rises, it becomes higher within you as well, not in the vessels, which are partly under your own control, nor in the phlegm of your more impassive organs, but in the capillaries: it rises, sucked up through these tubes into the outermost branches of your infinitely ramified being. Hither it mounts, here it passes out over you, rising higher than your breath, to which you flee as to your last stand. Ah! whither then, whither then? Your heart drives you out of yourself, your heart pursues you, and you are almost frantic, and you cannot get back inside yourself again. Like a beetle that has been trodden on, you gush out of yourself, and your slight surface hardness and adaptability go for nothing.

O empty night! O dim out-looking window! O carefully closed doors! Customs of immemorial standing, adopted, accepted, never quite understood. O silence in the stair-well, silence in the adjoining rooms, silence high up at the ceiling! O mother, O you only one, who put aside all this silence, once in my childhood. Who took it upon yourself, saying: 'Do not be afraid; it is I.' Who had the courage in the dead of night to be yourself the silence for the terror-stricken child, the child perishing with fear! You strike a light, and the noise is really you. And you hold the light before you and say: 'It is I; do not be afraid.' And you put it down, slowly, and there is no doubt: it is you; you are the light around these familiar, intimate things, that are there without afterthought, good, simple, unambiguous. And when something stirs in the wall, or a step is heard on the floor, you only smile, smile, transparent against the light background, on that fear-stricken face that looks searchingly at you, as if you were one, under seal of secrecy, with every muffled sound, in concert and agreement with it. Is there any power like your power among the rulers of the earth? See, kings themselves lie stiff and stark, and the teller of tales cannot distract them. Even on the happy bosoms of their mistresses terror creeps into them and makes them limp and impotent. But you come and keep the monstrous thing behind you, and put yourself in front of it wholly, not like a curtain it can lift up here and there. No! As if you had overtaken it at the call of one who needed you. As if you had come long, long before anything that may yet happen, and had behind you only the haste of your coming, your eternal path, the flight of your love.

*

THE moulder of plaster casts, before whose shop I pass every day, has hung two masks outside his door. The face of the young drowned woman, which was cast in the Morgue, because it was beautiful, because it smiled, smiled so deceptively, as though it knew. And beneath it, the face that did know. That hard knot of senses drawn tense; that unrelenting concentration of a music continually seeking to escape; the countenance of one whose ear a god had closed that he might hear no tones but his own, so that he might not be led astray by what is transient and confused in sounds, but in whom dwelt their clarity and enduringness; so that only soundless senses might bring in the world to him silently, a waiting world, expectant, unfinished, before the creation of sound.

Consummator of the world! As that which comes down in rain on the earth and the waters, falling down carelessly, falling by chance, inevitably rises again, joyous and less visible, out of all things, and ascends and floats and forms the heavens: so through you came the ascent of our downcast spirits and domed the world about with music.

Your music! it should have encircled the universe, not us alone. An organ should have been built for you in the Thebais, and an angel should have led you to that solitary instrument, through the desert mountain ranges, where kings repose and hetairæ and anchorites. And he should have flung himself up and away, fearful lest you begin.

Then you, O welling fountain, would have poured forth, unheard, giving back to the All that which only the All can endure. Bedouins would have swept past in the distance, superstitiously, but merchants would have flung themselves to the ground on the skirts of your music, as if you were the tempest. Only a few solitary lions would have prowled around you by night, far off, afraid of themselves, menaced by the stirrings of their own blood.

For who will now withhold you from lustful ears? Who will drive them from the concert halls, the venal company with sterile ears that prostitute themselves but never conceive? The seed streams forth, and they stand under it like sluts and play with it, or it falls, while they lie there in their abortive satisfaction, like the seed of Onan amongst them.

But, master, if ever a virginal spirit were to lie with unsleeping ear beside your music, he would die of blessedness, or he would conceive the infinite and his impregnated brain would burst with so great a birth.

*

I DO not think too lightly of the matter. I know it takes courage. But let us assume for a moment, that someone possesses it, this *courage de luxe* to follow them, in order to know for ever (for who could forget it again, or confuse it with anything else?) into what holes they creep afterwards and what they do with the rest of their long day and whether they sleep at night. That especially should be settled: whether they sleep. But more than courage is required. For they do not come and go like other people whom it is child's play to follow. They are here and away again, set down and carried off like lead soldiers. The places where they may be found are somewhat remote, but by no means hidden. The thickets disappear, the road takes a slight bend round the grass-plot: there they are, with a large, transparent space around them, as if they were under a glass case. You might mistake them for pensive pedestrians, these insignificant men, of slight, in every respect modest, build. But you would be wrong. Do you see the left hand grasping for something in the slanting pocket of an old overcoat; how it finds it and takes it out and holds the small object in the air, attracting attention with an awkward gesture? In less than a minute two, three birds appear, sparrows, that hop forward inquisitively. And if the man succeeds in conforming to their very precise idea of immobility, there is no reason why they should not approach still nearer. At last one of them flies up, and flutters a while nervously about the level of that hand which (O see!) holds out a little piece of stale, sweetened bread with unobtrusive, expressively renunciatory fingers. And the more people collect around him — at a suitable distance, of course — the less has he in common with them. He stands there like a candle in its sconce, that is dying out and sheds a light with what remains of wick and is all warm with it and has never stirred. And how he attracts, how he allures them, the many, little, stupid birds cannot tell at all. Were there no spectators, and were he allowed to stand there long enough, I am sure an angel would suddenly appear and, overcoming his repulsion, would eat the bit of stale, sweetened bread from that stunted hand. But now, as always, people are in the way. They take care that only birds come; they find that ample, and they assert that he expects nothing else. What else could it expect, this old, rain-battered scarecrow, stuck slightly awry in the earth like the figure-heads of ships in the little gardens at home? Does it, too, stand like that because it once stood forward somewhere in its life, where motion is greatest? Is it now so faded because it was once so gay? Will you ask it?

Only ask the women nothing when you see them feeding the birds. One could even follow them; it would be easy, for they do it merely in passing. But leave them alone. They do not know how it happens. All at once they have a large quantity of bread in their hand-bags, and hold out large pieces from under their worn cloaks, pieces that are a little chewed and moist. It does them good to think that their spittle will travel a little about the world, that the little birds will fly round with the taste of it in their mouths, even though naturally they will promptly forget it again.

*

THERE I sat before your books, headstrong man, try-ing to understand them as those others do who have not read them all together, but have picked out what appealed to them and been satisfied. For as yet I did not understand fame, that public destruction of one in process of becoming, into whose building-ground the mob breaks, displacing his stones.

Young man anywhere, in whom something stirs that makes you tremble, profit by the fact that no one knows you! And if they contradict you who hold you of no account, and if they abandon you entirely with whom you go about, and if they would destroy you because of your precious thoughts — what is this obvious danger, which holds you concentrated within yourself, compared to the later, subtle enmity of fame which leaves you harmless by scattering your forces?

Ask no one to speak of you, not even contemptuously. And when time passes and you find that your name is frequently on the lips of men, take it no more seriously than anything else that comes from those lips. Think rather that it has grown rank, and reject it. Take another name, any other, so that God may call you in the night. And conceal it from everyone.

Loneliest of men, withdrawn from all, how rapidly have they overtaken you by means of your fame! But lately they were fundamentally opposed to you, and now they treat you as their equal. And they carry your words about with them in the cages of their presumption and exhibit them in the streets and excite them a little from their own safe distance: all those wild beasts of yours.

When I first read you, they broke loose on me and assailed me in my wilderness — your desperate words — desperate, as you yourself became in the end, you whose course is wrongly traced on every chart. Like a fissure it crosses the heavens, this hopeless hyperbola of your path, that only once curves towards us and draws off again in terror. What mattered it to you whether a woman stays or goes, whether one is seized with vertigo and another with madness, whether the dead live, and the living appear to be dead: what mattered it? It was all so natural to you; you passed through it, as one might cross a vestibule, and did not stop. But yonder, within, you remained stooped, where our destiny seethes and settles and changes colour, farther in than anyone has yet been. A door had sprung open before you, and now you were among the alembics in the firelight. Yonder where, mistrustful, you took no one with you, yonder you sat and discerned processes of change. And there, since your blood drove you to reveal and not to fashion or to speak, there you conceived the vast project of magnifying single-handed these minutiæ, which you yourself first perceived only in test-tubes, so that they should be seen of thousands, immense, before all eyes. Then your theatre came into being. You could not wait until this almost spaceless life, condensed into fine drops by the weight of centuries, should be discovered by the other arts, and gradually made visible to the few who, little by little, come together in their understanding and finally demand to see the general confirmation of these extraordinary rumours in the semblance of the scene opened before them. For this you could not wait. You were there, and you had to determine and record the almost immeasurable: the rise of half a degree in a feeling; the angle of refraction, read off at close quarters, in a will depressed by an almost infinitesimal weight; the slight cloudiness in a drop of desire, and the well-nigh imperceptible change of colour in an atom of confidence. All these: for of just such processes life now consisted, our life, which had slipped into us and had drawn so deeply in that it was scarcely possible even to conjecture about it any more.

Given as you were to revelation, a timeless tragic poet, you had to translate this fine-spun activity at one stroke into the most convincing gestures, into the most present things. Then you set about that unexampled act of violence in your work, which sought ever more impatiently, ever more desperately, equivalents among things that are seen to the inward vision. There was a rabbit, a garret, a room where someone paced to and fro; there was the clatter of glass in a neighbouring apartment, a fire outside the windows; there was the sun. There was a church and a rock-strewn valley that was like a church. But that did not suffice; towers had ultimately to be brought in; and whole mountain ranges; and the avalanches that bury landscapes destroyed the stage, overladen with things tangible used for the sake of expressing the intangible. And now you could do no more. The two extremities that you had bent together, sprang apart; your mad strength escaped from the flexible shaft, and your work was as nothing.

Who should understand, otherwise, why in the

end you would not leave the window, headstrong as you always were? You wanted to see the passers-by; for the thought had occurred to you that some day one might make something out of them, if one decided to begin.

*

THEN for the first time did it strike me that one cannot say anything about a woman. I noticed when they spoke of her, how much they left out, how they mentioned other things — surroundings, localities, objects — and described them up to a certain point where they stopped, stopped quietly, and, as it were cautiously, just at the delicate outline, never retraced, which enclosed her. 'What was she like?' I would then ask. 'Fair, somewhat like you,' they would say, and would enumerate all sorts of additional details. But thereat she became quite indistinct again, and I could picture nothing more to myself. I was able really to *see* her only when Mother told me her story, a story I asked for again and again....

.... And every time she came to the scene with the dog, she used to close her eyes, and keep her rapt but quite translucent face, with a kind of eagerness, between her hands which cooled her temples with their touch. 'I saw it, Malte,' she declares, 'I saw it.' It was during her last years that I heard her tell this. At that time she no longer wanted to see anyone, and always carried with her, even on a journey, the small fine, silver sieve, through which she filtered everything she drank. She no longer took any solid food, save some biscuits or bread, which, when she was alone, she broke into small pieces and ate bit by bit, as children do crumbs. Her fear of needles at that time already dominated her completely. To others she simply said by way of excuse, 'I really cannot digest anything any more; but don't let that trouble you; I feel very well indeed.' But to me she would suddenly turn (for I was already a little bit grown-up) and say with a smile that cost her a severe effort, 'What a lot of needles there are, Malte, and how they lie about everywhere, and when you think how easily they might fall out....' She tried to say this playfully, but terror shook her at the thought of all the insecurely fastened needles which might at any instant, anywhere, fall into something.

*

But when she spoke of Ingeborg, then nothing could happen to her; then she did not spare herself; then she spoke louder, then she laughed at the memory of Ingeborg's laugh, then everyone should see how lovely Ingeborg had been.

'She made us all happy' she said, 'your father, too, Malte, literally happy. But afterwards, when we were told that she was going to die, although she seemed to be ailing only a little, and we all went about hiding the truth from her, she sat up one day in bed, and said to herself, like one who wants to hear how a thing sounds: "You mustn't put such a strain on yourselves; we all know it, and I can set your minds at rest; it is well just as it is; I want no more." Just imagine, she said: "I want no more"; she who made us all happy! Will you understand that some day when you are grown-up, Malte? Think about it in years to come; perhaps it will come to you. It would be well indeed, if there were someone who understood such things.'

'Such things' occupied Mother when she was alone, and she was always alone in these last years.

'I shall never really hit upon it, Malte,' she sometimes said with her strangely daring smile, which was not meant to be seen by anyone and served its whole purpose in being smiled. 'But what a pity no one is tempted to find an explanation! If I were a man — yes, just if I were a man — I would ponder over it, taking everything in due course and order and right from the beginning. For there must surely have been a beginning, and if one could only lay hold on that, it would at least be something. Ah! Malte, we pass away thus, and it seems to me people are all distracted and preoccupied and pay no real attention when we pass away. It is just as if a shooting-star fell and no one saw it and no one expressed a wish. Never forget to wish something for yourself, Malte. One should never give up wishing. I do not believe there is any fulfilment, but there are wishes that endure, that last a whole life long, so that, indeed, one could not wait for their fulfilment.'

Mother had had Ingeborg's small desk brought up and put in her own room. I often found her at it, for I could go in whenever I pleased. My step was completely silenced by the carpet, but she felt my presence, and stretched out one of her hands to me over the other shoulder. This hand had no weight, and to kiss it was like kissing the ivory crucifix that was held out to me before I went to sleep. At this low writing-desk with its lid open before her, she would sit as at some instrument. 'There is so much sun in it,' she would say, and in truth the interior was remarkably bright, with its old yellow lacquer, on which flowers were painted, alternately red and blue. And where there were three flowers together, a violet one separated the two others. These colours together with the green of the narrow, ornamentally carved border, were as dim as the background, without being actually distinct, was luminous. This resulted in an unusually subdued harmony of tones that stood in intimate relation to one another, without asserting themselves beyond that.

Mother drew out the little drawers, which were all empty.

'Ah! roses,' she said, bending forward a little towards the faint perfume that had not quite gone. She always imagined that something might yet be suddenly discovered in a secret drawer no one had thought of, which would yield only at the pressing of some hidden device. 'All at once it will spring forward, you shall see,' she said gravely and anxiously, and pulled rapidly at all the drawers. But all the papers that had actually been left in the drawers she had carefully folded and locked away without reading. 'I should not understand it in any case, Malte; it would certainly be too difficult for me.' She was convinced that everything was too complicated for her. 'There are no classes in life for beginners; it is always the most difficult thing that is asked of one first.' I was assured that she had become like this only after the terrible end of her sister, the Countess Ollegaard Skeel, who was burned to death as she sought to re-arrange the flowers in her hair before a ball, in front of a candle-lit mirror. But more recently it had been Ingeborg who seemed to her the most difficult of all to understand.

And now I shall write down the story as Mother told it when I asked her for it.

'It was in the middle of summer, on the Thursday after Ingeborg's funeral. From the place on the terrace where we were having tea, the gable of the family vault could be seen through the giant elms. The table had been set as if there had never been one more person sitting at it, and we had also spread ourselves out around it. And we had each brought something, a book or a work-basket, so that we were even a little crowded. Abelone (Mother's youngest sister) was pouring the tea, and we were all occupied handing things round, except your grandfather, who looked from his chair in the direction of the house. It was the hour when the post was expected, and it usually happened that Ingeborg brought the letters, as she was kept longer in the house than the others giving the orders for dinner. Now during the weeks of her illness we had had plenty of time to get accustomed to her not coming; for we knew, only too well, that she could not come. But that afternoon, Malte, when she really could not come any more...she came. Perhaps it was our fault; perhaps we called her. For I remember that all at once I sat there and tried to think what it really was that was now different. Suddenly it became impossible for me to say what it was; I had quite forgotten. I looked up and saw all the others turned towards the house, not in any special, striking way, but just calm and as usual in their expectancy. And I was just on the point (it makes me quite cold when I think about it, Malte) but, God help me, I was just on the point of saying: "Wherever is — ?" when Cavalier shot from under the table as he always did, and ran to meet her. I saw it, Malte; I saw it. He ran towards her, although she was not coming; for him she was coming. We understood that he was running to meet her. Twice he looked round at us, as if questioning. Then he rushed at her as he always did, just as he always did, Malte; and he reached her, for he began to jump round, Malte, round something that was not there, and then he leaped up on her, right up to lick her. We heard him whining for joy, and by the way he leaped up several times in quick succession you might have imagined he was hiding her from us with his gambols. But suddenly there was a howl, and whirling round from his own leap into the air, he dashed back with unaccustomed clumsiness, and lay stretched out before us, strangely flat, and never moved. From the other wing of the house the man-servant came out with the letters. He hesitated for a little; evidently it was not easy to walk towards our faces. Besides, your father had already motioned to him to stop. Your father, Malte, did not like animals; but, for all that, he now went up, slowly, as it seemed to me, and bent over the dog. He said something to the servant, something brief, monosyllabic. I saw the servant rush forward to lift Cavalier up; but your father took the dog himself, and carried it, as if he knew exactly where to take it, into the house.'

*

On one occasion, when it had grown almost dark as she told this story, I was on the point of telling Mother about *the hand*: at that moment I could have done it. I had already taken a long breath in order to begin; but then it struck me how well I understood the servant's not being able to approach their faces. And in spite of the waning light I feared what Mother's face would be like when she saw what I had seen. I quickly took another breath, to make it appear that that was all I had meant to do. A few years later, after the remarkable night in the gallery at Urnekloster, I went about for days with the intention of taking little Erik into my confidence. But after our nocturnal conversation he had once more shut himself completely away from me; he avoided me; I believe that he despised me. And just for this reason I wanted to tell him about *the hand*. I imagined I would rise in his estimation (and I wanted that keenly, I do not know why); if I could make him understand that I had really had that experience. But Erik was so clever in his evasions that I never got to the point. Besides, we left shortly afterwards. So, strangely enough, this is the first time that I am telling (and after all only for myself) of an occurrence that now lies far back in the days of my childhood.

How small I must still have been I see from the fact that I was kneeling on the stool in order to be within convenient reach of the table on which I was drawing. It was an evening in winter, in our apartment in town, if I am not mistaken. The table stood in my room, between the windows; there was no lamp in the room save that which threw its light on my papers and on Mademoiselle's book; for Mademoiselle sat next me, her chair pushed back a little, and was reading. She was always far away when she read; I do not know that she was absorbed in her book. She could read for hours, but she seldom turned the leaves, and I had the impression that the pages became steadily fuller and fuller, as if by looking she added words to them, certain words that she needed and which were not there. So it seemed to me as I went on drawing. I was drawing slowly, without any very decided intention, and when I stuck, I would survey the picture with my head bent a little to the right; in that position I always found out soonest what was lacking. There were officers on horseback, who were galloping to battle, or they were in the midst of the fray — which was far simpler, for in that case, almost all one needed to draw was the smoke that enveloped everything. Mother, it is true, always insists that they were islands I was painting — islands with large trees, and a château, and a stairway, and flowers on the bank that were supposed to be reflected in the water. But I think she is making that up, or this must have happened at a later time.

It is certain that on that particular evening I was drawing a knight, a solitary, easily recognisable knight, on a strikingly caparisoned horse. He became so gaily-coloured that I had to change my crayons frequently, but the red was most in demand, and for it I reached again and again. Once more I was about to seize it, when it rolled (I can see it yet) right across the illumined drawing-paper to the edge of the table and fell past me before I was able to stop it, and disappeared. I really needed it, and felt very annoyed at having to clamber down after it. Awkward as I was, I had to make all sorts of preparatory movements before I was able to do this. My legs seemed to me far too long, and I could not pull them out from under me; the prolonged kneeling had benumbed my limbs; I could not tell what was part of me, and what was part of the stool. At last I did get down, rather bewildered, and found myself on a fur pelt that stretched from under the table as far as the wall. But here a fresh difficulty arose. My eyes, accustomed to the brightness above and still excited by the colours on the white paper, were unable to distinguish anything beneath the table, where the blackness seemed to me so compact that I was afraid I should knock against it. I had therefore to depend on my sense of touch, and kneeling, supported on my left hand, I combed with my other hand the long cool hairs of the fur rug, which began to feel quite friendly, save that no pencil was to be found. I imagined I must be losing a good deal of time, and was about to call to Mademoiselle and ask her to hold the lamp for me, when I noticed that to my involuntarily strained eyes the darkness was gradually growing more penetrable. I could already distinguish the wall at the back, which ended in a prominent, bright moulding; I ascertained my position in relation to the legs of the table; above all I recognised my own outspread hand which, somewhat like an aquatic animal, was moving down there all alone, examining the ground. I watched it, as I remember still, almost with curiosity; it seemed as if it knew things I had never taught it, groping down there so independently, with movements I had never known it show before. I followed it up as it pressed forward; I was interested in it, ready for anything to happen. But how could I have been prepared to see suddenly come to meet it out of the wall another hand, a larger, extraordinarily thin hand, such as I had never beheld before! It came groping in similar fashion, from the other side, and the two outspread hands moved blindly towards one another. My curiosity was by no means satisfied, but it suddenly vanished, and only terror remained. I felt that one of the hands belonged to me, and that it was committing itself to some irreparable deed. With all the control I still possessed over it, I kept hold of it, and drew it back slowly on its flat, without taking my eyes off the other hand which went on groping. I realised that it would not cease to do this; and I cannot tell how I got up again. I sank deep into the chair; my teeth were chattering, and I had so little blood in my face that it seemed to me there could be no more blue in my eyes. 'Mademoiselle —' I wanted to say, but I could not. But she herself took fright, and, flinging her book away, knelt beside my chair and cried out my name; I believe she shook me. But I was perfectly conscious. I swallowed once or twice; for now I wanted to tell her.

But how? I made an indescribable effort to master myself; but it was impossible to express what had happened in any intelligible fashion. If there were words for such an occurrence, I was too young to find them. And suddenly the fear seized me that, in spite of my tender years, they would nevertheless all at once appear, these words, and it seemed to me more terrible than anything else to have to utter them then. To live through once again, differently, the reality I had experienced down there, to recite it from the beginning, to hear myself admitting it — for that I had not strength.

It is of course imagination on my part to say now that I already felt then that something had entered into my life, my particular life, with which I alone should have to go about always and always. I can see myself lying in my latticed bed, unable to sleep, somehow confusedly foreseeing that life would be like this: full of many special things that are meant for oneself alone and may not be spoken. Certain it is that a ponderous and melancholy pride gradually grew within me. I pictured myself going about, charged with inner secrets and in silence. I felt a passionate sympathy for older people; I admired them, and resolved to tell them that I admired them. I proposed to tell it to Mademoiselle at the next opportunity.

*

AND then came one of those illnesses that set themselves to prove to me that this was not my first private experience. The fever ransacked me and dragged up from the deeps adventures, images, facts, of which I had been ignorant: I lay there overwhelmed by myself, awaiting the moment when I should be bidden to set these all to rights again within me, carefully and in proper order. I began; but it all increased in my hands, it resisted me, there was much too much of it. Then rage seized me, and I flung everything in pell-mell, squeezing it together; but I could not close myself over it again. And then I cried, half-open as I was, I cried and cried. And when I began once more to look out from myself, they had been standing for a long time beside my bed holding my hands, and a candle was burning there, and their great shadows moved behind them. My father commanded me to say what was the matter. It was a friendly, gentle order, but an order nevertheless. And he became impatient when I did not reply.

Mother never came at night — or rather, she did come once. I had cried and cried, and Mademoiselle had come and Sieversen, the housekeeper, and Georg, the coachman; but that had been of no avail. And then finally they had sent the carriage for my parents, who were at a great ball, at the Crown Prince's, I think.

And all at once I heard the carriage driving into the courtyard, and I became quiet, sat up and watched the door. There was a slight rustling in the adjoining rooms, and Mother came in in her magnificent court robe, of which she took no care — almost ran in, letting her white fur fall behind her, and took me in her bare arms. With an astonishment and enchantment I had never experienced before, I touched her hair, her small, smooth face, the cool jewels in her ears, and the silk at the curve of her flower-scented shoulders. And we remained like this, weeping tenderly and kissing one another, until we felt that Father was there and that we must separate. 'He has a high fever,' I heard Mother say timidly; and my father took my hand and felt my pulse. He wore the uniform of a Master-of-the-Hunt with its lovely, broad, watered blue ribbon of the Order of the Elephant. 'What nonsense to send for us!' he said, speaking into the room without looking at me. They had promised to go back if there was nothing serious the matter; and there certainly was nothing serious. But I found Mother's dance-card on the cover of my bed, and white camellias, which I had never seen before and which I laid on my eyes when I felt how cool they were.

*

But it was the afternoons that were endless during such illnesses. In the morning after a bad night one always fell asleep, and when one wakened thinking it was morning again, it was really afternoon and remained afternoon and never ceased to be afternoon. So you lay there in the freshly-made bed, perhaps growing a little at the joints, but far too tired to imagine anything to yourself. The taste of apple-sauce lasted a long time, and the utmost you could do was somehow involuntarily to reconstruct this flavour and let its clean acidity circulate in you in place of thoughts. Later on, as strength returned, the pillows were propped up behind you, and you could sit up and play with soldiers; but they fell so easily on the sloping bed-tray and always a whole row at once, and as yet you had not sufficient vitality always to begin over again from the beginning. Suddenly you found the effort too much, and you asked to have everything taken away quickly, and it was good once more to see only your two hands, off there on the unencumbered coverlet.

When Mother sometimes came for half an hour and read me fairy tales (Sieversen came for the proper long reading); it was not for the sake of the stories themselves. For we agreed that we did not like fairy tales. We had a different conception of the wonderful. To us, things that happened naturally would always be the most wonderful. We set no great store on flying through the air, fairies disappointed us, and from being metamorphosed into something else, we expected but a very superficial change. But we did read a little, so as to appear occupied; we did not like, when anyone came in, to have to explain first what we were doing. Especially towards my father we were exaggeratedly explicit.

Only when we were quite sure we would not be

disturbed, and when darkness was gathering outside, did we abandon ourselves to memories, common memories which seemed old to both of us, and over which we smiled; for we had both grown up since then. We remembered that there was a time when Mother wished that I had been a little girl, and not the boy there was no use denying that I was. I had somehow guessed this, and I had hit upon the notion of knocking sometimes in the afternoon at Mother's door. Then when she asked who was there, I took delight in answering from outside, 'Sophie,' making my small voice so elegant that it tickled my throat. And when I entered then (in the small girlish house-dress which I always wore with its sleeves rolled all the way up), I was simply Sophie, Mother's little Sophie, busy about her household duties; and Mother had to plait a tress for her, so that she should not be mistaken for the naughty Malte, if ever he should return. This was by no means to be desired; his absence was as pleasant for Mother as for Sophie; and their conversations (carried on by Sophie always in the same high-pitched voice) consisted mostly in enumerations of Malte's misdeeds, complaints about him. 'Ah yes, that Malte!' Mother would sigh. And Sophie was well informed on the mischievousness of boys in general, as though she knew a whole lot about it.

'I should like very much to know what has become of Sophie,' Mother would suddenly say in the course of these recollections. On that point Malte could hardly give her any information. But when Mother suggested that Sophie must certainly be dead, he would stubbornly contradict her and implore her not to believe that, however little proof there might be to the contrary.

*

WHEN I reflect on it now, I never cease to wonder that I always managed wholly to return from the world of these fevers, and was able to adjust myself to that social existence, where each one wanted support in the feeling that he was among familiar people, and was careful to be on good terms with the comprehensible. If you looked forward to anything, it came or it did not come; there was no third possibility. There were things that were sad, altogether sad, and there were pleasant things, and a host of indifferent things. If there was an enjoyment destined for you, it was an enjoyment, and you had to conduct yourself accordingly. All this was essentially very simple, and if you had the key to this mode of existence it went of its own accord. For within these appointed boundaries everything found its place: the long monotony of the lesson-hours, when it was summer outside; the walks that had afterwards to be described in French; the visitors into whose presence you were summoned, who found you amusing just when you were sad, and who made merry over you as at the melancholy visage of certain birds that have no other face. And of course the birthday-parties, to which children were invited on your account whom you scarcely knew, shy children who made you shy, or rude children who scratched your face and broke the presents you had just received, and who suddenly departed when all the toys had been pulled out of the boxes and drawers and lay in heaps on the floor. But when you were playing alone, as usual, you might yet happen to pass inadvertently beyond the confines of this conventional, and on the whole harmless, world and find yourself among circumstances that were entirely different and by no means to be foreseen.

At times Mademoiselle had her migraine, which was unusually violent; and these were the days when it was difficult to find me. I know that on these occasions the coachman was sent to the park, when it occurred to my father to ask for me and I was not to be found. From one of the upper guest-rooms I could see him run out and call for me at the entrance to the long drive. These rooms were side by side in the gable of Ulsgaard and, as we had few visitors in those days, they were almost always unoccupied. But adjoining them was that great attic that had so strong an attraction for me. There was nothing to be seen in it save an old bust which, I believe, represented Admiral Juel; but the walls were covered right round by a succession of deep, grey wardrobes so that the window had had to be placed in the bare, white-washed space above them. I had found the key in one of the doors, and it opened all the others. In a short time I had examined them all: eighteenth-century chamberlains' coats, all chilly with their inwoven, silver threads, and the beautifully embroidered vests that were worn with them; costumes belonging to the Orders of the Dannebrog and the Elephant, so rich and heavy, and lined with material so soft to the touch, that one mistook them at first for women's dresses; then real robes, which, separate on their wicker stands, hung stiffly like marionettes from some play planned on too large a scale and now so entirely out-moded that the heads had been used for some other purpose. Alongside these were closets, in which it was dark, when they were opened, dark because of high-buttoning uniforms which looked much more worn than all the other things, and which really wished they had not been kept.

No one will find it surprising that I pulled all these out and took them to the light; that I held now this garment, now that, against me or flung it about my shoulders; that I hastily donned a costume which might fit me and, arrayed in it, ran curious and excited to the nearest guest-room, before the tall, narrow mirror composed of bits of irregularly green glass. Ah! how one trembled to be there, and how ravishing when one was! When out of the dimness something advanced, more slowly than oneself, for the mirror seemed incredulous and, somnolent as it was, unwilling to repeat immediately what had been said to it. But it had to in the end, of course. And now there appeared something surprising, strange, altogether different from one's expectation, something sudden, independent, which one rapidly surveyed, only in the next instant to recognise oneself, not without a trace of irony which came within a hairsbreadth of spoiling all the fun. But when one promptly began to talk and bow, to nod to oneself, to walk away, constantly looking round, and then come back, determined and exhilarated — then imagination was at hand as long as one wanted it.

It was then that I first experienced the influence which can emanate from a particular costume. Hardly had I donned one of these suits, when I had to admit that it had me in its power; that it prescribed my movements, the expression of my features, even, indeed, my ideas. My hand, over which the lace cuff fell and fell again, was anything but my usual hand; it moved like an actor; I might even say that it was watching itself, exaggerated though that sounds. These disguises never, indeed, went so far as to make me feel a stranger to myself: on the contrary, the more varied my transformations, the more assured was I of my own identity. I grew bolder and bolder, more and more ambitious; for my ability to recover myself was beyond all doubt. I did not apprehend the temptation in this rapidly growing security. My undoing came upon me when the last wardrobe, which I had not heretofore been able to open, yielded one day, to furnish me, not particular costumes, but all kinds of random paraphernalia for masquerades, the fantastic possibilities of which drove the blood to my head. It is impossible to recount all that I found there. In addition to a *baútta* which I remember, there were dominos in various colours, there were women's dresses, that tinkled brightly with the little coins with which they were sewn; there were pierrot-costumes that looked silly to me, and tucked Turkish trousers, and Persian fezzes from which little camphor sachets slipped out; and coronets garnished with stupid, expressionless

stones. All these I rather despised; they were so shab-
bily unreal; they hung there so empty and miserable,
and drooped so slack and helpless when they were
dragged out into the light. But what induced in me a
kind of intoxication were the capacious mantles, the
wraps, the shawls, and the veils, all those yielding,
wide, unused fabrics, that were so soft and caressing,
or so smooth that one could scarcely take hold of them,
or so light that they flew by one like a breath, or sim-
ply heavy with their own great weight. In them I
first discerned really unrestricted and endlessly varied
possibilities: I might be a slave-girl about to be sold,
or Joan of Arc, or an old king, or a wizard. All these
lay to my hand, especially as there were also masks,
large, threatening or astonished faces adorned with real
beards and thick or up-raised eyebrows. I had never
seen masks before, but I understood at once what masks
ought to be. I had to laugh when it occurred to me
that we had a dog who acted as if he wore one. I
recalled his affectionate eyes, that always seemed to be
looking out as from behind into his hirsute visage. I
was still laughing as I disguised myself, and I
completely forgot what I had intended to represent.
But no matter; it was a novel and exciting experience
to defer the decision until I should be standing before
the mirror. The face I fastened on had an odour that
made it feel singularly cavernous; it fitted closely to my
own face, but I was able to see through it quite com-
fortably. Then, when the mask was on, I selected vari-
ous kinds of scarves, which I bound about my head
like a turban, in such a way that the edge of the mask,

which reached downwards into an immense yellow cloak, was also almost entirely hidden on top and at the sides. At length, when I had exhausted my powers of invention, I considered myself sufficiently disguised. To complete the outfit I seized a large staff, which I held at my side, as far out as my arm could reach; and in this fashion, not without difficulty, but, as it seemed to me, full of dignity, I dragged myself along towards the mirror in the spare bedroom.

It was really magnificent, beyond all expectation. The mirror, too, gave it back instantly: it was too convincing. It would not have been at all necessary to move much; this apparition was perfect, even though it did nothing. But I wanted to discover what I actually was, so I turned round a little and finally raised both arms: large gestures, as if in the act of exorcism, were, I saw immediately, the only fitting ones. But just at this solemn moment, I heard quite near me, muffled by my disguise, a mixed and very complicated noise. Much frightened, I lost sight of the presence in the mirror and I was grievously disturbed to perceive that I had overturned a small round table laden with objects that were probably very fragile, though what they were Heaven alone knew. I bent down as well as I could, and found my worst fears confirmed: everything seemed to be in pieces. Two useless parrots of greenish-violet porcelain were of course shattered, each in a different, but equally malign, fashion. A box, from which rolled bonbons that looked like insects in silken chrysalids, had cast its cover a considerable distance away; only half of it was to be seen, the other half had quite disappeared. But most annoying of all, a scent-bottle had been shivered into a thousand tiny fragments, and from it there had been spilled some sort of old essence that now left a mark of very repulsive physiognomy on the spotless parquet. I wiped it up quickly with some of the stuff hanging about me, but it only became blacker and more unpleasant. I was, indeed, desperate. I picked myself up and tried to find something with which to repair the damage. But nothing was to be found. Besides I was so hampered, not only in my vision, but in my every movement, that my wrath rose against my absurd situation, which I no longer understood. I pulled at all the knots of my accoutrement; but that only made them tighter. The cords of the mantle were strangling me, and the stuff on my head was pressing down as though more and more were being added to it. Furthermore, the atmosphere had become heavy and as though mouldy with the stale odour of the spilled liquid.

Hot and angry, I rushed to the mirror and watched with difficulty through the mask the working of my hands. But just for this the mirror had been waiting. Its moment of revenge had come. While I strove with measurelessly increasing anguish to tear myself somehow out of my disguise, it forced me, by what means I know not, to lift my eyes, and imposed on me an image, nay, a reality, an alien, unbelievable, monstrous reality, with which, against my will, I became permeated: for now it was the stronger, and it was I who was the mirror. I stared at this great, terrifying, unknown personage before me, and it seemed appalling to me that I should be alone with him. But at the very moment I thought thus, the worst befell: I lost all knowledge of myself, I simply ceased to exist. For one second I had an unutterable, sad, and futile longing for myself, then there was only he — there was nothing but he.

I ran away from him, but now it was he that ran. He knocked against everything, he did not know the house, he had no idea where to go; he managed to get down a stair; he stumbled over someone in the passage who shouted in struggling free. A door opened, and several persons came out. Oh, oh, what a relief it was to recognise them! There were Sieversen, the good Sieversen, and the housemaid and the butler; now everything would be put right. But they did not spring forward to the rescue; their cruelty knew no bounds. They stood there and laughed; my God, they could stand there and laugh! I wept, but the mask did not let the tears escape; they ran down inside over my cheeks and dried at once, and ran and dried again. And at last I knelt before them, as no one has ever knelt before; I knelt, and lifted up my hands, and implored them, 'Take me out, if it is still possible, and keep hold of me!' But they did not hear; I had no longer any voice.

Sieversen used to tell to the day of her death, how I sank down and how they went on laughing, thinking it was part of the play. They were used to that kind of thing from me. But then I had continued to lie there and never answered a word. And their fright when they finally discovered that I had fainted, and lay prostrate in all those clothes, like a bundle of something, just like a bundle!

*

THE days passed with incalculable rapidity, and all at once the time had come again, when we must invite the pastor, Dr. Jespersen. This was the occasion of a repast, tiresome and interminable for everyone concerned. Accustomed to pious neighbours who were always overwhelmed by his presence, Dr. Jespersen was entirely out of his element with us; he was, so to speak, thrown on dry land and lay gasping. The gills he had developed for himself worked with difficulty; blisters formed, and the whole structure was endangered. Materials of conversation, to be exact, were non-existent; remainders were being disposed of at unbelievable prices; it was a liquidation of all assets. In our house Dr. Jespersen had to content himself with being a sort of private person; but that was exactly what he had never been. He had been, so far as he could think, appointed to the faculty of the soul. For him the soul was a public institution, which he represented, and he saw to it that he was never off duty, not even in his relations with his wife, 'his modest, faithful Rebecca, sanctified by the bearing of children,' as Lavater expressed it of another case.

(As for my father, his attitude to God was perfectly correct and faultlessly courteous. At church it sometimes seemed to me quite as though he were indeed Master-of-the-Hunt to God himself, when he stood there attentive or bowed his head. To Mother, on the contrary, it seemed almost offensive that anyone should maintain an attitude of politeness towards God. Had chance bestowed upon her a form of religion with expressive and complicated observances, it would have been a joy for her to kneel for hours, to prostrate herself and to make correctly the sign of the great cross, touching her breast and her shoulders. She did not actually teach me to pray, but it was a comfort to her to know that I kneeled willingly and clasped my hands, with fingers bent or upright as appeared to me more expressive. Left a good deal to myself, I passed early through a series of phases which I did not until much later, in a period of despair, connect with God; and then, indeed, with such violence that God was formed and shattered for me almost in the same moment. It is plain that after this I had to start all over again from the beginning. And for that beginning I often felt that I needed Mother, though naturally it was better to live through it alone. Besides which she had long been dead by that time.)*

Mother could treat Dr. Jespersen with an almost boisterous levity. She would begin conversations with him which he took seriously, and when he then heard himself speaking she thought she had done enough, and forgot him promptly as though he were already gone. 'However can he,' she sometimes said, 'go about and visit people just when they are dying!'

He came to see her also on that occasion; but she certainly no longer saw him. Her senses were expir-

* Written on the margin of the MS.

ing, one after the other, and the first to go was sight. It was in the autumn, and we ought already to have left for the city; but just then she fell ill, or rather she began at once to die, slowly and inconsolably to perish away over her whole body's surface. The doctors came, and one day they were all present together and took possession of the whole house. For several hours it seemed to belong to the Geheimrat and his assistants, as though we had no longer any say in things. But immediately after that they lost all interest, and came one at a time as from mere politeness, to take a cigar and a glass of port. And meanwhile Mother died.

There was only Mother's sole brother, Count Christian Brahe, yet to be expected, who, as will be remembered, had been for a time in the Turkish service, where he was always said to have gained great distinction. He arrived one morning, accompanied by a foreign servant, and I was surprised to see that he was taller than my father and apparently older as well. The two gentlemen at once exchanged a few words which, as I surmised, referred to Mother. A pause ensued. Then my father said: 'She is greatly disfigured.' I did not understand this expression, but I shivered when I heard it. I had the impression that my father, too, had to master himself before he uttered it. But it was probably his pride that suffered most in making this admission.

*

NOT until several years later did I hear further mention of Count Christian. That was at Urnekloster, and it was Mathilde Brahe who liked to talk about him. I am sure, however, that she coloured the various episodes of his career in a rather arbitrary fashion; for my uncle's life, which the public, and even our family, knew only through tales that he never took the trouble to contradict, offered boundless opportunities for embellishment. Urnekloster is now in his possession. But no one knows whether he is living there. Perhaps he is still travelling, as his habit was; perhaps the announcement of his death, written by his foreign servant in bad English or in some unknown tongue, is on its way at this moment from some remote part of the earth. Or perhaps this man will give no sign of life when one day he is left alone. Perhaps they have both disappeared long ago and only exist under assumed names in the passenger list of some missing ship.

Certain it is that when in those days a carriage drove into the courtyard of Urnekloster, I always expected to see him enter, and my heart began to beat in a peculiar manner. According to Mathilde Brahe, that is how he would come, suddenly turning up when one least thought it possible. He never came; but for weeks my imagination busied itself with him. I had the feeling that we ought to get into contact with one another, and I would like to have had some real knowledge of him.

When shortly after this, however, my interest veered round and as a result of certain events went over entirely to Christine Brahe, I did not, strangely enough, make any attempt to discover the circumstances of her life. On the contrary, I was troubled by the thought that her portrait might be among the paintings in the gallery. And the desire to make certain of this grew so insistent and tormenting, that for several nights I could not sleep, until, quite unexpectedly, there came that night on which, Heaven help me, I rose and went upstairs with my candle, which seemed to be afraid.

For my own part I had no thought of fear. I had no thought of anything; I simply went. The lofty doors yielded almost playfully before me, and above me the rooms through which I passed kept very still. And at last I noticed from the feeling of depth which came upon me like a breath, that I had entered the gallery. On my right hand I felt the windows with their nocturnal glimmer, and I knew that the pictures ought to be on my left. I lifted my candle as high as I could. Yes: there were the pictures.

At first I meant to look at the women only, but I soon recognised one portrait and then another, whose pendant hung at Ulsgaard; and when I illumined them thus from beneath, they moved and wanted to come into the light, and it seemed heartless of me not to give them time for that at least. There was Christian IV, again and again, with his beautifully braided queue along his broad, gradually rounded cheek. There were presumably his wives, of whom I knew only Christine Munk; and suddenly Frau Ellen Marsvin looked at me, suspicious in her widow's weeds and with that same string of pearls on the brim of her high hat.

There were King Christian's children, always different ones, the offspring of his successive wives: the 'incomparable' Eleonore, on a white pacing palfrey, in her heyday, before her ordeal. The Gyldenlöves: Hans Ulrik, of whom the Spanish ladies said that he painted his face, so full-blooded was he, and Ulrik Christian whom, once seen, one never again forgot. And nearly all the Ulfelds. And that one there, with one eye painted black, might well be Henrik Holck, who came to be Count of the Empire and Field Marshal at the age of thirty-three. It had happened thus: On his way to the damsel Hilleborg Krafse, he dreamed he was given a naked sword instead of a bride; and he took it to heart and turned back and began his brief and bold career, which ended with the plague. I knew them all. We also had at Ulsgaard the ambassadors to the Congress of Nimeguen, who all slightly resembled one another because they had all been painted at the same time, each with a little, cropped moustache like an eyebrow over the sensual, almost staring mouth. I need not say that I recognised Duke Ulrik and Otto Brahe and Claus Daa and Sten Rosensparre, the last of his race; for I had seen portraits of them all in the dining-room at Ulsgaard, or I had found in old portfolios copper-plate engravings that depicted them.

But then many were also there whom I had never seen; few women, but children were there. My arm had been tired for some time, and now it was shaking; yet I raised the light again and again in order to see the children. I understood them, those little girls each carrying a bird on her hand and forgetting all about it. Occasionally a small dog sat at their feet, a ball lay on the floor, fruit and flowers were on a table nearby; while on the pillar behind, there hung, minute and provisional, the coat-of-arms of the Grubbes, or the Billes, or the Rosenkrantzes. So many things had been gathered round them, as if a large indemnity were due them. But they stood there simply in their dresses, and waited; one saw that they were waiting. And that made me think of the women again and of Christine Brahe, and whether I should recognise her.

I wanted to run quickly to the end of the gallery and return thence looking for her, when I knocked against something. I turned so abruptly round that little Erik leaped back, whispering:

'Take care of your light!'

'You are there?' I said breathless, and I was not sure whether this was a good, or a thoroughly bad, omen. He only laughed and I did not know what would happen next. My light was flickering, and I could not rightly discern the expression on his face. Probably it was unfortunate that he was there. But then, drawing nearer to me, he said:

'*Her* portrait is not there; we are still always looking for it upstairs.'

With his low voice and his single moveable eye he made a kind of upward gesture. And I realised that he meant the attic. But suddenly a singular thought occurred to me.

'We?' I asked, 'Is she then upstairs?'

'Yes,' he nodded, standing very close to me.

'Is she looking for it, too?'

'Yes, we are looking.'

'Then the picture has been put away?'

'Yes, just imagine!' he said indignantly.

But I did not quite understand what she wanted with the picture.

'She wants to see herself,' he whispered, very near.

'Ah, yes,' I replied, as if I understood. At that he blew out my candle. I saw him stretching forward into the light with his eyebrows raised high. Then it was dark. I stepped back involuntarily.

'What are you doing?' I cried, stifled, and my throat was perfectly dry. He sprang towards me, and hung on my arm and giggled.

'What?' I asked harshly and tried to shake him off, but he clung fast. I could not prevent him from putting his arm round my neck.

'Shall I tell you?' he whispered between his teeth, and a little saliva spurted into my ear.

'Yes, yes, quickly!'

I was not aware of what I said. He was embracing me altogether now, stretching as he did so.

'I have brought her a looking-glass,' he said and giggled again.

'A looking-glass?'

'Yes, because her portrait is not there.'

'No, no,' I said.

Of a sudden he drew me nearer the window and pinched my forearm so sharply that I screamed.

'She is not in there,' he breathed into my ear.

Involuntarily I pushed him away; something within him cracked; I thought I had broken him.

'Go, go!' I said, and now I had to laugh myself. 'Not in there? How so, not in there?'

'You are stupid,' he answered sullenly, whispering no longer. His voice had changed register, as though he were beginning a new, and as yet unused, part of it. 'Either one is in there,' he pronounced with strict, precocious gravity, 'and in that case one is not here: or one is here, and cannot be in there.'

'Of course,' I answered quickly, without reflecting. I feared he might otherwise go away and leave me alone. I even stretched out my hand to touch him.

'Shall we be friends?' I proposed. He wanted to be urged.

'It's all the same to me,' he said curtly.

I attempted to inaugurate our friendship, but did not dare embrace him.

'Dear Erik,' I managed to say, gently touching him somewhere. I felt very tired all at once. I looked round; I no longer understood how I had come here or how it was that I had not been afraid. I did not rightly know where the windows were and where the pictures. And as we left he had to lead me.

'They won't do anything to you,' he assured me magnanimously and giggled again.

*

DEAR, dear Erik; perhaps you were after all my only friend. For I have never had one. It is a pity you set no store by friendship. I should have liked to tell you so many things. Perhaps we might have suited one another. One can never know. I recollect that your portrait was being painted at that time. Grandfather had got someone to come and paint you. An hour every morning. I cannot recall what the painter looked like; I have forgotten his name, although Mathilde Brahe used to repeat it every minute.

Did he see you as I see you? You wore a suit of heliotrope-coloured velvet. Mathilde Brahe adored that suit. But what does that matter now? I should only like to know whether he saw you. Let us assume that he was a real painter. Let us assume that it did not occur to him you might die before he should be done; that he did not treat his subject at all sentimentally; that he simply worked. That the dissimilarity of your two brown eyes fascinated him; that he was not for one moment ashamed of the immoveable one; that he had the discrimination not to place anything on the table beside your hand,· which was, perhaps, resting lightly on it —. Assuming everything else that may be necessary and giving it value, we have then a portrait, your portrait, the last in the gallery at Urnekloster.

(And when one departs, having seen them all, there is still that boy's picture there. One moment: who is that? A Brahe. Do you see the pale argent on the sable field and the peacock feathers? There is the name, too: Erik Brahe. Was there not an Erik Brahe who was condemned to death? Yes, of course, that is well enough known. But this cannot be the same. This boy died when he was quite young, no matter when. Can you not see that?)

*

WHEN visitors came and Erik was summoned, Fräulein Mathilde Brahe always asserted that his resemblance to the old Countess Brahe, my grandmother, was simply amazing. She must have been a very great lady. I did not know her. But I have a very vivid recollection of my father's mother, the real mistress of Ulsgaard. This, indeed, she always remained, however strongly she resented Mother's entering the house as the wife of the Master-of-the-Hunt. After that she constantly acted as though she were effacing herself, and referred the servants to Mother for every trivial detail, while in important matters she calmly made decisions herself and carried them out without consulting anyone. Mother, I imagine, did not wish it otherwise. She was so little fitted for the management of a large establishment; she entirely lacked the faculty of distinguishing between important and unimportant things. When a matter was mentioned to Mother, it always seemed to her of all-exclusive importance; in her absorption she forgot other things which after all still existed. She never complained about her mother-in-law. And to whom should she have complained? Father was an extremely respectful son, and Grandfather had little to say.

Frau Margarete Brigge had always been, as far as my recollection of her goes, a tall and unapproachable old lady. I cannot picture her except as much older than the chamberlain. She lived her life in our midst without the least consideration for anyone. She preserved her independence of us all; she had always about her a sort of lady-companion, the ageing Countess

Oxe, whom by some benefaction she had put under a boundless obligation. This must have been a singular exception in her life, for she was not given to good deeds. She did not like children, and no animals were allowed to come near her. I do not know whether there was anything else that she did like. It was said that as a very young girl, she had been engaged to the handsome Felix Lichnowski, who came to so cruel an end at Frankfort. And in fact, after her death a portrait of the prince was found, which, if I am not mistaken, was returned to his family. I am inclined to believe now that perhaps she had abandoned, for the retired country life which existence at Ulsgaard more and more became with the passing years, another and more brilliant career, the one for which nature had destined her. It is hard to say whether she regretted the life she had missed. Perhaps she despised it, because it had never come to her, because it had missed the opportunity of being lived with skill and talent. She had buried all this so deep within her, and had covered it with layers, many hard, brittle layers, of slightly metal-sheened shell, of which that for the time being uppermost appeared cool and new. Now and again, however, she betrayed by a naïve impatience that she thought she was not getting sufficient attention. In my time she would suddenly choke at table in some unconcealed and complicated fashion which assured her of the sympathy of all, and made her appear, for the moment at least, as sensational and as exciting as she would have liked to be in the larger sense. I suspect, however, that my father was the only one who took these much too frequent accidents seriously. He would look at her, bending politely forward, and one could see from his face that he was in thought offering her, so to speak, his own perfectly-conditioned wind-pipe, placing it entirely at her disposal. The chamberlain had naturally stopped eating, too; he took a sip of wine, and refrained from comment.

At table he had on one single occasion asserted his rights in opposition to his spouse. That had been long ago; yet the story was still retailed maliciously and in secret; almost everywhere there was someone who had never heard it. It was to the effect that there had been a time when the chamberlain's wife would fly into a passion about wine-stains that had through clumsiness been made on the table-cloth. Any such stain, whatever occasion might have provoked it, was always noted by her and exposed, one might say, under the severest rebuke. This had happened once when several distinguished guests were present. A few innocent stains, of which she made far too much, formed the subject of her sarcastic accusations; and though Grandfather tried his best to warn her by little signs and interpolated jocular remarks, she still persisted obstinately in her reproaches which a few minutes later, however, she was compelled to cut short in the middle of a sentence. For something unprecedented and absolutely incomprehensible occurred. The chamberlain had asked for the red wine which had just been passed around, and was now most attentively filling his own glass. Only, strangely enough, he did not cease pouring although the glass had long been full, but amid growing stillness continued to pour slowly and carefully, until Mother, who could never restrain herself, burst out laughing, and thus set right the whole affair by making a pleasantry of it. For everyone joined in, relieved, while the chamberlain looked up and handed the bottle to the servant.

Later another peculiarity got the upper hand of my grandmother. She could not bear anyone in the house to fall ill. Once when the cook had cut herself, and my grandmother happened to see her with her bandaged hand, she maintained that the whole house reeked of iodoform, and it was difficult to convince her that the woman could not be dismissed for that reason. She did not wish to be reminded of the possibility that she herself might fall ill. If anyone was imprudent enough to manifest some slight discomfort in her presence, she considered it nothing more nor less than a personal affront, and long bore the offender a grudge.

In the autumn of Mother's death, the chamberlain's wife shut herself up completely in her apartments with Sophie Oxe, and broke off all intercourse with us. Even her son was no longer admitted. It is true this death occurred most inconveniently. The rooms were cold, the stoves smoked, and the mice had thronged into the house — no place was safe from them. But it was not only that: Frau Margarete Brigge was indignant that Mother was dying; that there should stand on the order of the day a subject about which she declined to speak; that the young wife should take precedence of her, when she certainly meant to die herself, though she had not yet finally set the day. For she often reflected on the fact that she would have to die. But she was not going to be hurried. She would, of course, die when it pleased her, and then all the others could go ahead and die after her, if they were in such haste.

She never quite forgave us Mother's death. She also aged very rapidly during the following winter. When she walked she was as tall as ever, but she drooped in her arm-chair, and her hearing grew harder. One could sit beside her and stare her straight in the face for hours; she never took the slightest notice. She was somewhere within herself; she returned only rarely and for brief moments to her empty senses which she no longer inhabited. Then she would say a few words to the Countess, who adjusted her shawl, and with her large, freshly-washed hands would draw in her dress, as if water had been spilled or as if we were not quite clean.

She died on the approach of spring, one night, in the city. Sophie Oxe, whose door stood open, had heard nothing. When they found Margarete Brigge in the morning she was as cold as glass.

Immediately after that the chamberlain's severe and terrible disease set in. It was as if he had awaited her end, that he might die as inconsiderately as he was destined to.

*

It was in the year after Mother's death that I took notice of Abelone for the first time. Abelone was al-

ways there. This did her great harm. And then Abelone
was unsympathetic — as I had once ascertained a good
while before, and I had since never seriously put that
opinion to the test. It would have seemed until now
almost ludicrous to me to inquire into the nature of
my relations with Abelone. Abelone was there, and
one made use of her as best one could. But all at once
I asked myself: 'Why is Abelone here?' Each of us
had a reason to be there, even if it was not always as
obvious, as, for example, the utility of Fräulein Oxe.
But why was Abelone there? For a while there had
been some talk of her seeking diversion. But that had
passed into oblivion. No one contributed to Abelone's
diversion, and she certainly did not give one the impres-
sion of being diverted.

Besides, Abelone had one gift: she sang. That is
to say, there were times when she sang. There was a
powerful and unswerving music in her. If it is true
that angels are masculine, then one may well say there
was something masculine in her voice, a radiant, celes-
tial masculinity. I, who even as a child had been so
distrustful of music (not because it lifted me out of my-
self more violently than anything else, but because I
had noticed that it never let me resume the level at
which it found me, but set me lower down, somewhere
deep in the region of the unachieved), I endured this
music: on it one could ascend upright, ever higher
and higher, until one imagined that for the last little
while this must very nearly have been Heaven. I did
not then suspect that Abelone was to open yet other
heavens for me.

At first our relationship consisted in her telling me of the days of Mother's girlhood. She was anxious to show me how valiant and youthful Mother had been. There was no one at that time, she assured me, to compare with Mother in dancing or riding. 'She was most daring and quite tireless, and then all at once she married,' said Abelone, still amazed after so many years. 'It happened so unexpectedly, no one could really understand it.'

I was curious to know why Abelone had not married. She appeared to me comparatively old, and that she might still do so never occurred to me.

'There was no one there,' she answered simply; and as she said it she became really beautiful. 'Is Abelone beautiful?' I asked myself in surprise. Then I left home to go to the Academy for the Sons of the Nobility, and an odious and painful period of my life began. But yonder at Sorö, when I stood in the embrasure of a window, apart from the others, left by them for a little in peace, I would look out on the trees; and at such moments, and at night, there grew in me the certainty that Abelone was beautiful. And I began to write her all those letters, some long, some short, many secret letters, in which I thought I was speaking of Ulsgaard, and of my unhappiness. But, as I can see now, they must really have been love-letters. For the holidays came at last, though it seemed as if they never would, and then it was as if by pre-arrangement that we did not meet in the presence of the others.

Nothing whatever had been agreed upon between

us, but when the carriage turned into the park I could not refrain from getting out, perhaps simply because I did not wish to drive up to the house like any stranger. Summer was already at its height. I took one of the side paths and ran towards a laburnum tree. And there was Abelone. Beautiful, beautiful Abelone!

I shall never forget how it was when you looked at me; how you wore that look, holding it up on your back-tilted face like something that was not fixed.

Ah! has not the climate changed at all, has it not grown milder round about Ulsgaard with all our warmth? Do not certain roses bloom longer now in the park, even into December?

I shall tell nothing about you, Abelone. Not because we deceived one another — since even then you loved one whom you, loving one, have never forgotten, and I loved all women — but because only harm would come from the telling.

*

THERE are tapestries here, Abelone, wall tapestries. I imagine that you are here; six tapestries there are: come, let us pass slowly before them. But first step back, and see them all at once. How peaceful they are, are they not? There is little variety in them. There is always that oval, blue island, floating on a background of modest red, which is decked with flowers and inhabited by tiny animals busy with their own affairs. Only yonder, in the last hanging, the island rises a little, as if it had grown lighter. It has always one figure on it, a lady, in various costumes, but she is always the same. Sometimes there is a smaller figure beside her, a maid-servant; and heraldic animals are always there, large, also on the island, taking part in the action. On the left there is a lion, and, conspicuous on the right, a unicorn. They carry the same pennants which show high above them: three silver moons ascendant, in blue chevrons on a red field. Have you looked? Will you begin with the first?

She is feeding a falcon. How sumptuous her raiment is! The bird is on her gloved hand and it stirs. She is watching it and at the same time plunging her hand into the bowl the handmaid brings, to offer it something. Below, on the right, a silken-haired dog is lying on the train of her dress, looking up and hoping it will be remembered. And, did you notice? a low rose-trellis shuts off the island at the back. The blazoned animals stand erect, with heraldic arrogance. The coat-of-arms is repeated as a mantle enveloping them. A handsome clasp holds it together. It floats.

Do we not involuntarily approach the next tapestry more softly, when we see how profoundly the lady is absorbed? She is weaving a garland, a small, round crown of flowers. Thoughtfully she chooses the colour of the next carnation in the flat basin the servant holds for her, while she fastens the one just selected in its place in the wreath. Behind her on a seat there stands unused a basket full of roses, which a monkey has uncovered. But this time they must be carnations. The lion no longer takes part; but the unicorn on the right understands.

Should not music enter into this stillness, is it not already there, subdued? Gravely and quietly adorned, she has gone forward (how slowly, has she not?) to the portable organ, and now stands playing it. The pipes separate her from the maid-servant who is blowing the bellows on the other side of the instrument. She has never yet been so lovely. Wonderfully her hair is brought forward in two plaits, fastened together over the head-dress in such a way that the ends rise out of the knot like a short crest. The lion, out of humour, unwillingly endures the sounds, biting back a howl. But the unicorn is beautiful, as with an undulating motion.

The island has become broader. A tent has been set up. Of blue damask and flaming gold. The animals hold it open, and she is stepping forward, homely almost in her queenly attire. For what are her pearls compared with herself? The maid has opened a small casket, and now lifts from it a chain, a ponderous, magnificent ornament that has always been kept under lock and key. The little dog sits beside her on a high place prepared for it, and looks on. Have you discovered the motto on the upper edge of the tent? It is: *A mon seul désir.*

What has happened? Why is the little rabbit running down there, and why does one see at once that it is running? Everything is in such suspense. The lion has nothing to do. She herself holds the banner. Or is she leaning on it? With her other hand she has grasped the horn of the unicorn. Is this mourning? Can mourning stand so straight? And can a mourning-garment be so mute as that green-black velvet with its lustreless folds?

But here is yet another festival; no one is invited to it. Expectation plays no part in it. Everything is here. Everything for ever. The lion looks round almost threateningly: no one may come. We have never seen her weary before; is she weary? Or is she merely resting because she holds something heavy? A monstrance, one might say. But she curves her other arm towards the unicorn, and the flattered animal bridles and rears and leans against her lap. It is a mirror that she holds. See! She is showing the unicorn its likeness —.

Abelone, I imagine that you are here. Do you understand, Abelone? I think you must understand.

PART TWO

EVEN the tapestries of the *Dame à la Licorne* are now no longer in the old château of Brissac. The time has come for houses to part with everything; they can keep nothing any more. Danger has become more certain than security. No scion of the Delle Vistes walks beside you with these things in his blood. They have all passed away. No one speaks your name, Pierre d'Aubusson, grandest Grand Master of an ancient house, at whose behest, perhaps, these pictures were woven that exalt everything and prostitute nothing. (Ah! Why have poets ever written otherwise about women, more literally, as they imagined? Certain it is, we might know no more than is presented here.) Now one comes upon them by chance, among chance comers, and is almost frightened to be here uninvited. But there are others passing by, though they are never many. The young people scarcely even halt before them, unless somehow their studies oblige them to have seen these things once, because of some particular characteristic they possess.

Young girls one does occasionally find before them. For in museums there are many young girls who have left the houses that can no longer keep anything. They find themselves before these tapestries and forget themselves a little. They have always felt that such a life must have existed — a quiet life of leisurely gestures, never quite defined; and they remember dimly that for a time they even believed this life would be their own. But then they quickly bring out a sketch-book and begin to draw, whatever it may be — one of the flowers or a little happy animal. What exactly it is, they have been told, does not matter. And it really does not matter. The essential thing is that they shall draw; for with this intent they one day left their home, rather impetuously. They are of good family. But when they lift their arms as they sketch, it is evident that their dress has not been fastened at the back or, at any rate, not entirely. There are some buttons they cannot reach. For when the dress was made, no one imagined that they would suddenly go away alone. In a family there is always someone to help with such buttons. But here, good heavens! who is going to bother about it in so large a city? Unless, perhaps, one has a girl friend; but friends are in the same quandary, and so in the end it would come to their buttoning each other's dresses. That is ridiculous; it would remind one of the family, of which one does not want to be reminded.

But inevitably they wonder sometimes as they draw, whether it would not have been possible to remain at home. If only one could have been religious, sincerely religious, in step with the others! But it seemed so absurd to try being religious in common.

The path has somehow become narrower: families can no longer approach God. So there remained only certain other things that might at need be shared. But then, if the division was fairly made, so shamefully little came to each person; and if deception were practised in it, disputes arose. No, it is really better to sketch, no matter what. In time some resemblance will appear; and Art, especially when one acquires it thus gradually, is after all a truly enviable possession.

And in their intense absorption with the task they have undertaken, these young women, they never lift their eyes. They do not perceive that with all their strenuous copying they do nothing save to suppress within themselves the unalterable life opened before them, radiant and endlessly ineffable, in these woven pictures. They do not want to believe it. Now that so many things are different, they, too, want to change. They are on the verge of abandoning themselves, and of thinking about themselves as men might speak of them when they are not present. To them that seems progress. They are already nearly convinced that life, if one would not stupidly lose it, consists in the search for one enjoyment and then another, and again, another, that is yet more keen. They have already begun to look about, to search — they, whose strength has always lain in their being found.

That comes, I believe, of their weariness. For centuries now, women have undertaken the entire task of love; they have always played the whole dialogue, both parts. For man has only echoed them, and badly. And has made the learning difficult with his inattention, with his neglect, with his jealousy, which is also a form of neglect. And they have nevertheless persevered day and night, and have grown in love and misery. And from among them, under the stress of endless need, have gone forth those valiant lovers, who, while they called him, rose above their man; who grew beyond him when he did not return, like Gaspara Stampa or like the Portuguese nun, who never desisted until their torture was transmuted into an austere, icy splendour which nothing could confine. We know about one and another because of letters, which as by a miracle have been preserved, or books of poems written in accusation or lament, or portraits in some gallery that look at us through a longing to weep which the painter caught because he knew not what it was. But there have been innumerably many more: Those who burned their letters, and others who had no strength left to write them. Aged women, grown hard, but with a kernel of delight which they kept hidden. Uncouth, powerful women, who, made strong through exhaustion, let themselves grow gradually like their husbands, and who were yet entirely different in their inmost being, there where their love had laboured in the dark. Child-bearing women who never wanted to conceive, and who, when they finally died after their eighth child, had the gestures and the lightness of young girls looking forward to love. And those women who remained with their bullies and drunkards because they had found the means, in themselves, to withdraw far from them as they could nowhere else; and this they could not conceal, when they came among people, but were radiant as though they moved always with the blessed. Who can say how many they were, or who they were? It is as if they had destroyed beforehand the words in which they might be described.

*

But now that so much is being changed, is it not time that we should change? Could we not try to develop ourselves a little, slowly and gradually take upon ourselves our share in the labour of love? We have been spared all its hardship, and so it has slipped in among our distractions, as into a child's drawer of toys sometimes a piece of real lace falls and pleases him and pleases him no longer and finally lies there among torn and dismembered things, worse than any of them. We have been spoiled by easy enjoyment, like all dilettanti, and are looked upon as masters. But what if we despised our successes, what if we began from the beginning to learn the work of love which has always been done for us? What if we were to go and become neophytes, now that so much is changing?

*

Now I know, too, what happened when Mother unrolled the little pieces of lace. For she had taken for her own use only one of the drawers in Ingeborg's desk.

'Shall we look at them Malte?' she would say; and she was as joyful as if she were about to be given everything the yellow-lacquered cabinet contained.

And then, for sheer impatience, she could not possibly unfasten the tissue-paper. I had to do that for her every time. But I, too, was greatly excited when the laces made their appearance. They were rolled on a wooden bobbin which was not to be seen for all the laces wound about it. Then we would unroll them slowly and watch the designs as they opened out, and were always a little scared when one of them came to an end. They stopped so suddenly.

First came strips of Italian work, tough pieces with drawn threads, in which everything was interminably repeated, as obviously as in a peasant's garden. Then all at once, our view would be shut off by a succession of grille-works of Venetian needle-point, as though we had been cloistered or imprisoned. But it opened again, and we looked deep into gardens that grew more and more artificial, until everything was as murky and warm to the eyes as in a hot-house; stately plants which we did not recognise opened their gigantic leaves, tendrils groped dizzily for one another, and the great open blossoms of the point d'Alençon dimmed everything with their scattered pollen. Suddenly, all weary and confused, we stepped out into the long track of the Valenciennes, and it was winter and early morning and hoar frost was on the ground. And we pushed through the snow-covered bushes of the Binche, and came to places where no one had been before; the branches hung so strangely downward, there might well have been a grave beneath them — but that we concealed from each other. The cold pressed ever more closely upon us, and at last, when the very fine pillow-lace came, Mother said: 'Oh! now we shall get frost-flowers on our eyes!' and so it was, too, for within us it was very warm.

We both sighed when the laces had to be rolled up again. It was a lengthy task, but we were not willing to entrust it to anyone else.

'Just imagine if we had had to make them!' said Mother, looking really frightened. I could not imagine that at all. I caught myself thinking of little insects incessantly spinning these things, and who, on that account, are left in peace. No, of course, they were women!

'They have surely gone to Heaven, those who made it,' I said, admiringly. I remember it occurred to me that for a long time now I had not asked any questions about Heaven. Mother drew a long breath; the laces once more lay rolled together.

After a little while, when I had already forgotten about it, she said slowly: 'In Heaven? I believe they are in the very heart of it. If one sees it so, that may well be eternal beatitude. One knows so little about it.'

*

OFTEN, when visitors came, it was said that the Schulins were retrenching. Their large, old manor-house had burned down some years previously, and they were now living in the two narrow wings and retrenching. But the habit of having guests was in their blood; they could not give it up. If someone arrived at our house unexpectedly, he probably came from the

Schulins; and if one of our visitors suddenly looked at his watch and hastened away in his fright, he was sure to be expected at Lystager.

By that time Mother really never went anywhere, but this the Schulins could not comprehend: there was nothing for it but one day to drive over and see them. It was in December, after some early falls of snow; the sleigh was ordered for three o'clock, and I was to accompany my father and Mother. But we never started punctually. Mother, who did not like having the carriage announced, usually came down much too soon, and when she found no one there, something always occurred to her that ought to have been done long ago, and she would begin looking about or putting things to rights somewhere upstairs, so that she could hardly be found again. Finally we would all stand there waiting. And when at last she was seated in the sleigh and tucked in, it appeared that something had been forgotten, and Sieversen would have to be fetched, for only Sieversen knew where it was. But then we would suddenly drive off, before Sieversen returned.

It had never really quite cleared off that day. The trees stood as if they could advance no further in the mist, and there was something perverse about driving into it. Meantime the snow had again begun silently to fall, and now it was as though the last of the scene had been blotted out and we were driving into a white sheet. There was nothing but the sound of the sleigh-bells, and one could not say where it actually came from. At one moment it ceased, as if the last tinkle had been sounded; but then it gathered itself up again, all together, and poured forth anew in full measure. One might have imagined one saw the church tower on the left; but suddenly the outline of the park wall appeared, high up, almost on top of us, and we found ourselves in the long avenue. The tinkling of the bells no longer ceased abruptly; it seemed to hang in clusters right and left on the trees. Then we swung in and drove around something, passed something else on the right, and came to a halt in the centre.

Georg had quite forgotten that the house was no longer there, and for all of us at that moment it was there. We ascended the front steps that led up to the old terrace, and only wondered at finding all in darkness. Suddenly a door opened below and behind us on the left, and someone cried, 'This way!' at the same time lifting and swinging a dim lantern. My father laughed: 'We are wandering about here like ghosts,' and he helped us down the steps again.

'But still there was a house there just now,' said Mother, and could not accustom herself so quickly to Viera Schulin, who warm and laughing had come running out to us. So we had to go in with her quickly, and the house was not to be thought of any longer. Our wraps were taken off in a small ante-room, and immediately we were in the midst of things, among the lamps, facing the heat.

These Schulins were an able race of independent women. I do not know if there were any sons. I only remember three sisters. The eldest had married a Marchese in Naples, whom she was at that time slowly divorcing, by process of several lawsuits. Then came Zoë, about whom it was said that there was nothing she did not know. And above all there was Viera, this warm Viera; God knows what has become of her. The Countess, a Narishkin, was really a fourth sister and in certain respects the youngest. The good Count Schulin felt as though he were married to all these ladies, and he came and went and kissed them at random.

Just then he was laughing heartily and he greeted us most courteously. I was passed around among the ladies, who pawed and questioned me. But I had firmly resolved, as soon as that was over, to slip out somehow and look for the house. I was convinced it was still there today. To get out of the room was not so difficult; one could creep along down among all their skirts like a dog, and the door of the ante-room was still on the latch. But the outer door would not yield. There were several contrivances on it of chains and locks, which I could not manage properly in my hurry. Yet it did suddenly open, but with a loud noise, and before I could get outside I was seized and drawn back.

'Stop! You can't slip away like that here!' cried Viera Schulin merrily. She bent over me, and I resolved to reveal nothing to this warm and laughing person. But as I did not say anything she took it for granted that a natural need had driven me to the door. She seized my hand, and had already started to walk, intending, half confidential and half condescending, to take me somewhere. This intimate misunderstanding wounded me beyond measure. I tore myself loose and looked angrily at her.

'It is the house I want to see,' I said proudly. She did not understand.

'The large house outside by the stairs.'

'Goose,' she said, snatching at me, 'there is no house there any more.'

I insisted that there was.

'We'll go sometime by daylight,' she proposed, to conciliate me. 'You can't go wandering round there at this hour. There are holes there, and just behind are father's fish-ponds which aren't allowed to freeze. You'll fall in and be turned into a fish.'

Therewith she pushed me before her, back again into the brightly-lit room. There they all sat and were talking, and I contemplated them one after the other. 'Of course they only go when it is not there,' I thought contemptuously; 'if Mother and I lived here, it would always be there.' Mother looked distraught, while the others were all talking at once. She was certainly thinking of the house.

Zoë sat down beside me and began to ask me questions. She had well-regulated features which showed from time to time a renewed glance of intelligence, as though she were always in the act of comprehending something. My father sat leaning a little to the right, listening to the Marchioness, who was laughing. Count Schulin stood between Mother and his wife and was relating some incident. But I saw the Countess interrupt him in the middle of a sentence.

'No, child, you are imagining that,' said the Count

good-humouredly, but his face, as he stretched forward above the two ladies, had all at once become as anxious as his wife's. The Countess, however, was not to be persuaded so easily out of her so-called imagination. She wore a very strained look, like someone who does not wish to be disturbed. She made slight, defensive movements with her soft, beringed hands. Somebody said 'Sst!' and suddenly there was complete silence.

Behind the people in the room the immense pieces of furniture from the old house pressed forward, much too close. The ponderous family silver shone and bulged as though it were being seen through a magnifying glass. My father looked round in surprise.

'Mamma smells something,' said Viera Schulin behind him, 'so we all have to be quiet; she smells with her ears.' But she herself stood, with raised eyebrows, attentive and all nose.

In this regard the Schulins had become a little peculiar since the fire. In the close, over-heated rooms an odour might rise at any moment, and then everyone would analyse it and express his opinion. Zoë, practical and conscientious, did something to the stove; the Count went here and there, stopped for a little at each corner of the room and waited; then said, 'It is not here.' The Countess had risen and did not know where to search. My father turned slowly right round on his heels, as if he had the smell behind him. The Marchioness, who had promptly assumed that it was an offensive smell, held her handkerchief over her mouth and looked at each one in turn to see if it had gone. 'Here, here!' cried Viera, from time to time, as if she had it. And around each word there was a strange silence. As for me, I had bravely exercised my sense of smell, too. But all at once (was it the heat of the room or the nearness of so many lights?) I was over-taken for the first time in my life by something akin to the fear of ghosts. It became clear to me that all these distinct grown people, who, just a minute before had been talking and laughing, were going about bent down and busy with something invisible; that they ad-mitted something was there which they did not see. And it was frightful that this thing should be stronger than them all.

My fear increased. It seemed to me that what they were seeking might break out on me like an eruption, and then they would see it and point to me. Utterly desperate, I looked across to Mother. She sat there extraordinarily erect; it seemed to me that she was waiting for me. I had scarcely reached her side, and perceived that she was trembling inwardly, when I knew that only now the house was beginning to dis-appear again.

'Malte, coward!' someone said with a laugh. It was Viera's voice. But we did not let go of one another and endured it together. We remained like that, Mother and I, until the house had again quite vanished.

*

YET it was the birthdays that were richest in almost incomprehensible experiences. One had, of course, already learned that life took pleasure in making no distinctions; but on this day one arose with a right to joy which was not to be doubted. Probably the sense of this right had been very early developed in one, at the stage when one grasps at everything and obtains it too, when, with unerring imaginative power, one invests those objects one happens to possess with the colourful intensity of one's then prevailing desire.

But suddenly come those remarkable birthdays when, fully established in the consciousness of this right, you see others becoming uncertain. You would like to be dressed as before, and then take to yourself all that follows. But you are hardly awake when someone shouts outside your bedroom door that the cake hasn't arrived yet; or you hear something break as the presents are being arranged on the table in the next room; or somebody comes in and leaves the door open, and you see everything before you should have seen it. That is the moment when something like an operation is performed on you: a brief but atrociously painful incision. But the hand that does it is experienced and steady. It is quickly over. And you have scarce got over it when you no longer think about yourself; you must rescue the birthday, watch the others, anticipate their mistakes, and confirm them in the illusion that they are managing everything admirably. They do not make it easy for you; they appear to be of an unexampled clumsiness, almost stupid. They contrive to come in with parcels of some sort that are destined for other people; you run to meet them and have afterwards to make it appear as if you had been running about the room for exercise, not for any special purpose. They want to surprise you and with a very superficial pretence of expectation open the lowest layer of a toy-box, which contains nothing more, only cotton-wool; then you have to relieve them of their embarrassment. Or, if it is a mechanical toy they are giving you, they break the spring themselves the first time they wind it up. It is therefore useful to practise beforehand, pushing along an overwound mouse, or the like, surreptitiously with your foot; in this way you can often deceive them and help them out of their confusion.

You managed all these things as they were demanded of you; it required no special ability. Talent was really necessary only when someone had taken pains and, overflowing with importance and good-humour, brought you a gift, and you saw even at a distance that it was a gift meant for somebody quite different from you, an entirely unsuitable gift; you did not even know anyone for whom it would have done, so unsuitable was it.

*

THE telling of stories, the real telling, must have been before my time. I have never heard anyone tell stories. At the time Abelone spoke to me of Mother's youth, it was evident that she could not tell them. Old Count Brahe was supposed still to be able to do so. I will write down here what Abelone knew of the story.

As a very young girl she must have been for

a time susceptible to a wide and curious variety of emotions. The Brahes lived in town at that period, in the Bredgade, and moved a good deal in society. When she came up to her room late at night she would think she was tired like the others. But then all at once she became aware of the window, and, if I understood her aright, she could stand looking at the night for hours, thinking: this concerns me. 'I stood there like a prisoner,' she said, 'and the stars were freedom.' At that time she was able to fall asleep without growing heavy. The expression 'falling asleep' was by no means appropriate to this season of her young maidenhood. Sleep was something that ascended with you, and from time to time your eyes were open and you lay on a new surface, not yet by any means the highest. And then you were up before dawn; even in winter, when the others came in sleepy and late to the late breakfast. In the evenings when darkness fell, there were, of course, only lights meant for the whole household, common lights. But those two candles that you lit quite early in the new darkness with which everything began again — these you had to yourself. They stood in their low double sconce, and shone peacefully through the small, oval shades of tulle, painted with roses, which had to be lowered from time to time. There was nothing inconvenient in that; for once you were in absolutely no hurry; and then it so happened you had to look up occasionally and reflect, when you were writing at a letter or in the diary, which had been begun some time previously in quite another hand, timorous and beautiful.

Count Brahe lived entirely apart from his daughters. He considered it mere fancy when anyone pretended to share his life with others. ('Hm, share —,' he would say.) But he was not displeased when people spoke to him of his daughters; he would listen attentively, as though they were living in another town.

It was therefore something entirely out of the ordinary when one day after breakfast he signed to Abelone to come to him. 'We have the same habits, it seems. I, too, get up early in the morning to write. You can help me.' Abelone still remembered as if it had been yesterday.

The next morning she was led into her father's study, admittance into which was looked upon as forbidden. She had no time to look about her, for she had to sit down at once opposite the Count at the writing-table, which looked to her like a vast plain with books and piles of papers for the villages.

The Count dictated. Those who asserted that Count Brahe was writing his memoirs were not altogether wrong. But these were not the political and military memoirs that were so eagerly awaited. 'I forget those things,' said the old gentleman curtly, when anyone broached these questions to him. But what he did not wish to forget was his childhood. To this he clung. And it was quite natural, according to him, that this very distant time should have the upper hand in him now, and that as he turned his gaze inwards, it should lie there, as in a clear, northern summer night, ecstatic and unsleeping.

Sometimes he sprang up and talked at the candles

so that they flickered. Or whole sentences had to be scored out, and then he would pace violently to and fro, his old, Nile-green dressing-gown waving about him. During all this there was yet another person present, Sten, the Count's aged servitor, a Jutlander, whose duty it was, when my grandfather sprang up, to lay his hands smartly on the loose papers covered with memoranda that lay scattered about the table. His Grace had the idea that the paper of that day was worthless, that it was much too light and flew away at the slightest breath. And Sten, the long upper half only of whose body could be seen, shared this distrust and seemed to squat on his hands, blind in the daylight and as grave as an owl.

This Sten spent his Sunday afternoons reading Swedenborg, and none of the domestics dared enter his room because he was supposed to be conjuring up spirits. Sten's family had always trafficked with spirits, and Sten was especially predestined to this commerce. An apparition had appeared to his mother on the night he was born. Sten had large, round eyes, and the other end of his gaze seemed to come to rest somewhere behind the person at whom he was looking. Abelone's father often asked after the spirits, as one would enquire about the health of someone's relatives. 'Are they coming, Sten?' he would ask benevolently. 'It is good if they will come.'

The dictating went its way for several mornings. But then one day Abelone could not spell 'Eckernförde.' It was a proper name, and she had never heard it before. The Count, who in truth had long been seeking a pretext for giving up the writing, which was too slow for his recollections, showed irritation.

'She cannot spell it,' he said sharply, 'and others will not be able to read it. And will they *see* at all what I am saying?' he went on angrily, keeping his eyes fixed on Abelone. 'Will they see him, this Saint-Germain?' he shrieked at her. 'Did we say Saint-Germain? Strike it out! Write: the Marquis de Belmare!'

Abelone struck out and wrote. But the Count continued to speak so rapidly that it was impossible to keep up with him.

'He could not endure children, this excellent Belmare, but he took me on his knee, small as I was, and I had the idea of biting his diamond buttons. That pleased him. He laughed, and lifted my chin until we were looking into each other's eyes. "You have splendid teeth," he said, "teeth that are enterprising. . . ." But I was noticing his eyes. I have gone about a good deal since then, and I have seen all kinds of eyes; but, believe me, such eyes never again. For these eyes a thing did not need to be present; it was there within them. You have heard of Venice? Very well. I tell you these eyes would have seen Venice here into this room, so that it would have been there as plain as that table. I sat one day in the corner of the room listening as he spoke to my father about Persia — sometimes I think my hands still smell of it. My father thought highly of him and his Highness the Landgrave was, in a way, his disciple. But naturally enough there were those who reproached him with believing in the past only when it was within himself. They could not understand that the whole business has no meaning unless one has been born with it....

'Books are empty,' cried the Count, turning towards the walls with a gesture of fury, 'it is blood that matters, it is in blood that we must learn to read. He had marvellous histories and strange pictures in his blood, this Belmare; he could open it where he pleased, something was always written there; not a page had been left blank. And when he shut himself up from time to time and turned the leaves in solitude, he came to the passages about alchemy and about precious stones and about colours. Why should not all these things have been there? They must surely be somewhere.

'He might easily have been able to live with a truth, this man, had he been by himself. But it was no trifle to live alone with a truth like his; and he was not so lacking in taste as to invite others to come and visit him when he was in her company; she should not enter the conversation: he was far too Oriental for that. "Adieu, Madame," he said to her sincerely, "until another time. Perhaps in another thousand years we shall be somewhat stronger and less disturbed." "Your beauty is just beginning to blossom, Madame," he said, and this was no mere polite speech. With that he went off and laid out his botanical park for the people, a kind of Jardin d'Acclimatation for the larger kind of lies, which had never been seen in our latitudes, and a palm-house of exaggerations, and a small, well-tended *figuerie* of false secrets. Then people came from everywhere, and he went about with diamond buckles on his shoes and was entirely at the disposal of his guests.

'A superficial existence, you say? Nevertheless it was essentially chivalrous towards his lady, and it allowed him to keep his years very well.'

For some time now the old man had no longer been addressing Abelone, whom he had forgotten. He paced to and fro like a madman and threw challenging glances at Sten, as if Sten were going to be transformed at a given moment into the person about whom he was thinking. But Sten had not yet been transformed.

'One had to see him,' the Count went on, obsessed. 'There was a time when he was perfectly visible, although in many cities the letters he received were not addressed to anyone: they bore simply the name of the town, nothing else. But I saw him.

'He was not handsome.' The Count gave a strangely hurried laugh. 'Nor was he even what people would call important or distinguished; there were always more distinguished men about him. He was wealthy, but in his case wealth was merely incidental and not to be depended on. He was well grown, although others carried themselves better. Of course I could not tell then whether he was clever, or this, that and the other to which we attach value — but he *was*.'

The Count, trembling, stood up and made a movement as if to fix something in space, conclusively.

At that instant he became aware of Abelone.

'Do you see him?' he asked her, imperiously. And

suddenly he seized one of the silver candlesticks and held the blinding light before her face.

Abelone remembered that she had seen him.

On the following days Abelone was summoned regularly, and after this incident the dictation proceeded much more quietly. The Count was putting together from all kinds of documents his earliest recollections of the Bernstorff circle, in which his father had played a definite part. Abelone had now adjusted herself so well to the peculiarities of her task that anyone seeing the two together might easily have mistaken their purposeful collaboration for real intimacy.

One day when Abelone was preparing to retire, the old gentleman approached her as though he were holding a surprise in his hands behind his back. 'Tomorrow we shall write about Julie Reventlow,' he said, savouring his words, 'she was a saint.'

Probably Abelone looked at him incredulously.

'Yes, yes,' he insisted in a commanding tone, 'such things are possible; there are still saints, Countess Abel.'

He took Abelone's hands and opened them as one opens a book.

'She had the stigmata,' he said, 'here and here.' And with his cold finger he tapped hard and sharp on both her palms.

Abelone did not know the meaning of the word 'stigmata.' It would be explained later, she thought; she was very impatient to hear about the saint whom her father had actually seen. But she was not summoned again, neither the next morning nor later....

'The Countess Reventlow has often been mentioned in your family since then,' concluded Abelone briefly when I asked her to tell me more. She looked tired; she maintained, too, that she had forgotten most of these events. 'But I still feel the two marks sometimes,' she said, smiling, and could not drop the thought and looked almost with curiosity at her empty hands.

*

EVEN before my father's death everything had changed. Ulsgaard was no longer in our possession. My father died in a town, in a flat that seemed alien and almost hostile to me. I had already gone abroad at the time and returned too late.

They had laid him on a bier, between two rows of candles, in a room that gave on the courtyard. The perfume of the flowers was bewildering; like many voices sounding all at once. His handsome face, in which the eyes were closed, wore an expression of courteous endeavour to recollect something. He was clothed in his uniform of Master-of-the-Hunt; but for some reason or other the white ribbon had been substituted for the blue. His hands were not folded; they lay obliquely crossed and looked artificial and meaningless. I had been hurriedly told that he had suffered a great deal: nothing of that was to be seen. His features were set in order like the furniture in a guest-room which some visitor has just left. I had the feeling that I had often seen him dead: I knew it all so well. The surroundings alone were new, and unpleasantly so. This oppressive room was new, with windows opposite that were probably the windows of other people. It was new that Sieversen should come in from time to time and do nothing. Sieversen had grown old. Then I was bidden to breakfast. More than once the meal was announced. I had no desire for breakfast that day. I did not realise that they wanted to get me out of the room. In the end, as I did not go, Sieversen somehow gave me to understand that the doctors were in the house. I did not see why. There was still something to be done, said Sieversen, looking at me intently with her reddened eyes. Then two gentlemen entered somewhat precipitately; they were the doctors. The first lowered his head with a jerk, as if he had horns and were going to butt, in order to look at us over his glasses: first at Sieversen, then at me.

He bowed with the stiff formality of a student. 'The Master-of-the-Hunt had one other wish,' he said in a tone exactly similar to his manner of entering the room; again one felt his precipitancy. I somehow compelled him to direct his look through his spectacles. His colleague was a stoutish, thin-skinned, blonde man; I thought it would be easy to make him blush. Then a pause ensued. It seemed strange that the Master-of-the-Hunt should still have wishes.

I involuntarily looked again at the fine, regular countenance. And I knew then that he wanted certainty. Fundamentally he had always desired certainty. Now he was about to have it.

'You are here for the perforation of the heart: please proceed.'

I bowed and stepped back. The two doctors acknowledged my courtesy simultaneously, and began at once to confer about their work. Someone was already pushing the candles aside. But the elder of the two doctors again took a few paces towards me. At a certain point, in order to spare himself the last part of the distance, he stretched forward and looked at me angrily.

'It is not necessary,' he said, 'that is to say, I think it would perhaps be better, if you . . .'

He seemed to me neglected and shabby in his so sparing and hurried movements. I bowed once more; circumstances ordained that I should already bow again.

'Thanks,' I said shortly, 'I shall not disturb you.'

I knew that I could endure the ordeal, and that there was no reason for my withdrawing from it. It was inevitable. Perhaps it would give me the key to the meaning of it all. Besides, I had never before seen how it is when someone's breast is pierced. It seemed to me in order not to evade so rare an experience, when it came without compulsion and without conditions. In disappointment I really no longer believed, even then; so there was nothing to fear.

No, no, nothing in the world can one imagine beforehand, not the least thing. Every occurrence is made up of so many separate details that cannot be foreseen. They are passed over in the act of imagining, which takes place so rapidly that one does not notice they are lacking. But the realities are slow and indescribably detailed.

Who, for example, would have thought of that

resistance? The broad, high breast had scarcely been laid bare when the hurried little man had found the spot he was seeking. But the instrument which he rapidly applied did not penetrate. I had the feeling that suddenly all time had gone from the room. We seemed like a group in a picture. But then time came rushing back and overtook us with a slight, gliding sound, and there was more of it than could be used. Suddenly there was knocking somewhere: I had never heard such knocking before — a warm, firm, double knocking. My ear transmitted it to my brain, and at the same time I saw that the doctor had driven his instrument home. But it took a little while before the two impressions coincided within me. So, I thought, it is done now. The knocking, so far as its tempo was concerned, sounded almost malicious.

I looked at the man whom I seemed to have known so long. No, he was in complete command of himself: a gentleman working swiftly and well, who had to leave immediately. He showed no trace of enjoyment or satisfaction in his handiwork. Only from some ancient instinct a few hairs had stood up on his left temple. He carefully withdrew the instrument, and there was left something resembling a mouth, from which twice in succession blood escaped, as if it were pronouncing a word in two syllables. The young, blonde doctor with an elegant gesture took it up quickly on a piece of cotton. And then the wound remained at peace, like a closed eye.

It is to be assumed that I bowed once more, without knowing, this time, quite what I was doing. At any rate I was astonished to find myself alone. Some-one had put the uniform in order again, and the white ribbon lay across it as before. But now the Master-of-the-Hunt was dead, and not he alone. Now his heart had been pierced, our heart, the heart of our race. Now it had passed. This, then was the shattering of the helm: 'Today Brigge and nevermore,' something said within me.

Of my own heart I did not think. But when it occurred to me later, I knew for the first time quite certainly that for this purpose it did not come in question. It was an individual heart. It was already on its way, beginning over again from the beginning.

*

I KNOW that I thought I should not be able to set out again at once. Everything must first be put in order, I said to myself over and over. What needed to be put in order was not quite clear to me. There was almost nothing to be done. I walked about the town and noticed that it had changed. I found it pleasant to observe, when I went out of the hotel in which I was staying, that it was now a town for grown people, showing itself off to you almost as to a stranger. Every-thing had shrunk a little, and I walked out the Lange-linie to the lighthouse and back again. When I reached the neighbourhood of the Amaliengade it was natural that an influence to which one had been subject for years should emanate from somewhere and attempt to exercise its old power again. In that part of the town there were certain corner-windows and porches and lanterns which knew a great deal about you and menaced you with that knowledge. I looked them straight in the face and let them know that I was staying at the Hotel Phoenix and could leave again at any moment. But even so my conscience was not at rest. I began to suspect that none of these influences and associations had really been mastered. I had one day secretly abandoned them, all unfinished as they were. So one's childhood also would have to be lived through to a finish, unless one were willing to regard it as lost for ever. And, while I understood how I lost it, I felt at the same time that I would never have anything else to which I could appeal.

I spent a few hours every day in the Dronningens Tvaergade, in those confined rooms that had the injured look of all apartments in which someone has died. I went to and fro between the writing-table and the big white porcelain stove, burning the Master-of-the-Hunt's papers. I had begun by throwing the letters into the fire in bundles just as I found them; but the little packets were too firmly tied and only charred at the edges. It cost me an effort to untie them. Most of them had a strong, penetrating scent which assailed me as though it wished to awaken memories in me, too. I had none. Then some photographs, heavier than the rest, happened to slip out; these photographs took an incredibly long time to burn. I do not know how it was, but suddenly I imagined that Ingeborg's likeness might be among them. But each time I looked I saw women, mature, magnificent, evidently beautiful, who suggested a different train of thought to me. For it presently appeared that I was not altogether devoid of memories after all. In just such eyes as these I had sometimes seen myself when, as a growing boy, I used to accompany my father along the streets. Then from the interior of a passing carriage they would envelope me with a look from which I could scarcely escape. Now I knew that they were comparing me with him and that the comparison was not in my favour. Certainly not; the Master-of-the-Hunt had no need to fear comparisons.

Perhaps I now know of something that he did fear. Let me tell how I came to this assumption. At the bottom of his portfolio there was a paper that had been folded for a long time, friable, broken at the folds. I read it before I burned it. It was in his most careful script, firmly and regularly written; but I noticed at once that it was only a copy.

'Three hours before his death,' it began and it referred to Christian IV. I cannot, of course, reproduce the contents verbatim. Three hours before his death he wished to get up. The doctor and Wormius, the valet, helped him to his feet. He stood somewhat unsteadily, but he stood, and they put on his quilted dressing-gown. Then he sat down suddenly on the edge of the bed and said something which they could not understand. The doctor kept constant hold of the king's left hand to prevent him from sinking back on the bed. So they sat, and from time to time the king spoke, thick and laboured, this unintelligible thing. At length the doctor began to encourage him and talk to him; he hoped gradually to discover what the king was trying to say. After a little the king interrupted him and said, all at once quite distinctly, 'O doctor, doctor, what is his name?' The doctor had some difficulty in remembering.

'Sperling, most gracious majesty.'

But this was really not the important thing. The king, as soon as he heard that they understood him, opened wide his right eye, the one he could still use, and expressed with all his features the single word his tongue had been forming for hours, the sole word that still existed: 'Döden,' he said, 'Döden.' *

There was no more on the sheet. I read it several times before I burned it. And I remembered that my father had suffered a great deal at the last. So they had told me.

*

SINCE then I have reflected a good deal on the fear of death, not without taking into consideration, in that connection, certain personal experiences of my own. I believe that I can really say I have felt it. It has overtaken me in the busy town, in the midst of people, often without any reason. But often, too, there have been abundant reasons. When, for example, a person sitting on a bench passed suddenly away, and the others all stood round and looked at him, and he was already far beyond the reach of fear: then I had his fear. Or that time, in Naples: that young girl who sat opposite me in the tram and died. At first it looked as if she had only fainted; for a while we even drove on.

* (Death, death.)

But soon there was no doubt that we had to stop. And behind us the vehicles halted, massed together, as though there would never be any more traffic in that direction. The pale, stout girl might have died peacefully, leaning against the person beside her. But her mother would not permit that. She contrived all possible difficulties. She disordered her clothes and poured something into her mouth which could no longer retain anything. She rubbed her forehead with a liquid someone had brought, and when the eyes, at that, rolled back a little, she began to shake her to make them look straight again. She shouted into those eyes that heard nothing: she worried the girl's whole body and pulled it to and fro like a doll, and finally she raised her arm and slapped the puffy face with all her might, so that she should not die. That time I was afraid.

But I had already been afraid before. For example, when my dog died, the one who accused me once and for all. He was very ill. I had been kneeling beside him the whole day, when he suddenly gave a short, jerky bark in the way he was accustomed to do when any stranger entered. A bark like that was a kind of signal arranged between us for such occasions, and I glanced involuntarily at the door. But it was already in him. I looked anxiously into his eyes, and he, too, looked into mine; but not to bid me farewell. His look was hard and hostile. He reproached me with having allowed it to enter. He was certain I could have prevented it. It was now clear that he had always overrated me. And there was no time left to explain to him. He continued to gaze at me, estranged and solitary, until the end came.

Or I was afraid when in autumn, after the first night frosts, the flies came into the room and revived once again in its warmth. They were singularly dried-up and took fright at their own buzzing; one could see they did not quite know what they were doing. They sat there motionless for hours and gave themselves up as lost until it occurred to them that they were still alive; then they flung themselves blindly in every direction, not knowing what to do when they got there, and one could hear them falling down again, here and there and everywhere. And finally they crawled about, and slowly died all over the room.

But even when I was alone I could be afraid. Why should I pretend that those nights had never been, when in fear of death I sat up, clinging to the fact that the mere act of sitting was at any rate a part of life: that the dead did not sit. This always happened in one of those chance rooms which promptly left me in the lurch when things went wrong, as if they feared to be taken to task and become involved in my misdeeds. There I sat, probably looking so dreadful that nothing had the courage to fraternise with me; not even the candle, which I had just done the service of lighting it, would acknowledge me. It burned away there by itself, as in an empty room. My last hope then was always the window. I imagined that outside there something might still be that belonged to me, even now, even in this sudden destitution of death. But scarcely had I looked thither when I wanted the window to be barricaded and blocked up like a wall. For now I knew that things were going on out there in the same indifferent way, that out there, too, there was nothing but my loneliness — the loneliness I had brought upon myself, to the greatness of which my spirit was no longer equal. I recalled people from whom I once had parted, and I did not understand how one could forsake human beings.

My God, my God, if any such nights await me in the future, leave me at least one of those thoughts that I have sometimes been able to pursue! It is not unreasonable, this that I ask; for I know that they were born of my fear just because my fear was so great. When I was a boy, they struck me in the face and told me I was a coward. That was because my fear was still unworthy. Since then, however, I have learned to be afraid with real fear, the fear that increases only when the power that creates it increases. We have no idea of this power, except in our fear. For it is so utterly inconceivable, so totally opposed to us, that our brain disintegrates at the point where we strain ourselves to think about it. And yet, for some time now I have believed that it is *ours,* this power, all our own, but that it is still too great for us. It is true that we do not know it; but is it not just our very own of which we know the least? Sometimes I reflect on how Heaven came to be and death; we have thrust away from us that which is most precious, because there were so many other things to do beforehand and because, being so busy, we could not keep it safely by us. And now much time has passed, and we have become accustomed to less worthy things. We no longer recognise that which is our own, and we are terrified by its supreme greatness. May that not be?

*

MOREOVER I now understood very well how one could carry with one, through all the years, deep in one's portfolio, the description of a dying hour. It need not even be an especially selected one; they all possess something almost rare. Can one not, for example, imagine somebody copying out the description of Felix Arvers' death? It took place in a hospital. He was dying with ease and tranquillity, and the sister, perhaps, thought he had gone further with it than he really had. In a very loud voice she called out an order, indicating where such and such was to be found. She was hardly an educated nun, and had never seen written the word 'corridor,' which at the moment she could not avoid using; thus it happened that she said 'collidor,' thinking it ought to be pronounced so. At that Arvers thrust death from him. He felt it necessary to put this right first. He became perfectly lucid and explained to her that it ought to be pronounced 'corridor.' Then he died. He was a poet and hated the approximate; or perhaps he was simply concerned with the truth; or it annoyed him to carry away this last impression that the world would go on so carelessly. That can no longer be decided. Only let no one think that he acted in a spirit of pedantry. Otherwise the same reproach would fall on the saintly Jean-de-Dieu, who sprang up in the midst of his dying and arrived just in time to cut down a man who had hanged himself in his garden, knowledge of whom had in some amazing fashion penetrated the inward tension of his agony. He, too, was concerned only with the truth.

*

THERE exists a creature, perfectly harmless when you see it; you scarcely notice it and forget it again immediately. But as soon as it manages somehow to get unseen into your ears, it develops there; it hatches, as it were, and cases have been known where it has penetrated into the brain and has thriven devastatingly, like those pneumococci in dogs that gain entrance through the nose.

This creature is one's neighbour.

Now since I have been knocking about alone like this, I have had innumerable neighbours; neighbours above me and beneath me, neighbours on my right and on my left, sometimes all four kinds at once. I might simply write the history of my neighbours; that would be the work of a lifetime. It is true that it would be, rather, the history of the symptoms of maladies they have caused in me. But it is a characteristic which they share with all creatures of similar nature, that their presence can be traced only through the disturbances they produce in certain tissues.

I have had irregular neighbours and others who were extremely regular. I have sat long endeavouring to discover the law of the former class; for it is evident that they, too, have a law. And when my punctual neighbours failed to come in at the usual time of night, I have tried to imagine what could have happened to them, and kept my light burning and been as anxious as a newly-married wife. I have had neighbours who were moved by sheer hatred, and neighbours who were involved in violent love-affairs; and I have experienced the sudden metamorphosis of one type into the other in the dead of night, and then, of course, sleep was no longer to be thought of. Indeed, one could observe in general that sleep is much less frequent than is supposed. My two Petersburg neighbours, for example, attached very little importance to sleep. One of them stood and played the fiddle, and I am sure that as he did so he looked across into the too wakeful houses opposite which never ceased to be illumined during those unbelievable August nights. Of my other neighbour on the right I knew at least that he lay in bed; during my time he never got up at all. He even had his eyes shut, but it could not be said that he slept. He lay and recited long poems, poems by Pushkin and Nekrassov, with the cadence in which children recite when it is demanded of them. And despite the music of my neighbour on the left, it was this fellow with his poem who wove a cocoon in my brain, and God knows what would have hatched out of it had not the student who occasionally visited him one day mistaken the door. He told me the story of his friend, and it turned out on the whole to be reassuring. At any rate, it was an artless, unambiguous tale that destroyed the teeming maggots of my conjectures.

This petty functionary, my neighbour, had had one Sunday the idea of solving a singular problem. He assumed that he was going to live a considerable time, say, another fifty years. The generosity he thus showed towards himself put him in a radiant humour. But he now sought to surpass himself. He reflected that these years could be changed into days, hours, minutes, indeed, if one persevered, into seconds; and he calculated and calculated, and the result was a total such as he had never seen before. It made him giddy; he had to rest a little. Time was precious, he had always heard, and he was amazed that a person possessing such a quantity of time was not continually being guarded. How easy it would be to steal him! But then his good, almost exuberant humour came back again; he put on his fur coat, to look a little broader and more imposing, and presented himself with the whole of this fabulous capital, addressing himself a trifle condescendingly:

'Nikolai Kusmitch,' he said benevolently and imagined himself also sitting without the fur coat, thin and miserable on the horse-hair sofa, 'I trust, Nikolai Kusmitch,' he said, 'that you will not pride yourself on your wealth. Always remember that money is not the chief thing. There are poor people who are thoroughly respectable; there are even impoverished members of the nobility and generals' daughters, who go about peddling things on the streets.' And the benefactor cited a number of other cases known to the whole town.

The other Nikolai Kusmitch, the one on the horse-hair sofa, the fortunate one, did not, so far, look in the least haughty; one might safely assume he would be reasonable. In fact, he altered nothing in his modest, regular mode of living, and he now employed his Sundays in settling his accounts. But after a few weeks it struck him that he was spending an incredible amount. 'I must retrench,' he thought. He rose earlier; he washed less thoroughly; he drank his tea standing; he ran to his office and arrived much too soon. He saved a little time in everything. But when Sunday came nothing of his savings remained. Then he realised that he had been duped. 'I should never have changed it,' he said to himself. 'How long a fine, unbroken year would have lasted! But this confounded small change, it disappears, one doesn't know how.' And there came an ugly afternoon, which he passed sitting in the corner of the sofa and waiting for the gentleman in the fur coat, from whom he meant to demand the return of his time. He would bolt the door and not allow him to depart until he paid up. 'In notes,' he would say, 'of ten years, if you please.' Four notes of ten, and one of five, and the remainder he could keep in the devil's name! Yes, he was ready to let him have the rest, provided he made no difficulties. Exasperated he sat on the horse-hair sofa and waited; but the gentleman never came. And he, Nikolai Kusmitch, who had so easily seen himself sitting there a few weeks before, was unable, now that he really sat there, to picture to himself the other Nikolai Kusmitch, the gentleman in the fur coat, the generous gentleman. Heaven knew what had become of him; probably his defalcations had been traced, and he was now sitting locked up somewhere. Surely he had not brought misfortune to him alone. Such swindlers always work on a large scale.

It occurred to him that there must be a state institution, a kind of Time Bank, where he might exchange part at least of his shabby seconds. After all, they were genuine. He had never heard of such an institution, but he was sure to find something of the sort in the directory under 'T.' Or perhaps it was called 'Bank for Time,' in which case one could easily look under 'B.' As a last resort the letter 'I' might be considered, too, for presumably it would be an Imperial Bank; that would accord with its importance.

Later Nikolai Kusmitch used always to assert that, although he was naturally in a depressed mood, he had not been drinking anything on that Sunday evening. He was therefore perfectly sober, when the following incident occurred, so far as one can tell at all what did happen then. Perhaps he had taken a little nap in the corner of his sofa; that was always possible. This short sleep gave him, at first, the greatest relief. 'I have been meddling with figures,' he said to himself. 'Now I have no head for figures. It is plain, however, that too great importance should not be attached to them. They are, after all, only a state arrangement, so to speak, made in the interests of good order. No one has seen them anywhere except on paper. The possibility, for example, of meeting a seven or a twenty-five in society is excluded. That simply does not happen. And so, from pure inadvertence, this slight confusion has taken place between Time and Money, as though the two could not be kept distinct.' Nikolai Kusmitch almost laughed. It was really excellent thus to have discovered the trick, and in good time, that was the essential thing, in good time. Now it would be different. Time was certainly a very annoying thing. But was he the only one thus afflicted? Did time not break up into seconds, just as he had experienced it, for others as well, even when they were not aware of the fact?

Nikolai Kusmitch was not altogether free from a malicious joy. 'Let it...' he was just about to think, when a strange thing happened. He suddenly felt a breath on his face; it blew past his ears; he felt it on his hands. He opened his eyes wide. The window was securely shut. And as he sat there in the dark room with wide-opened eyes, he began to realise that what he was now feeling was real time, passing by. He recognised them actually, these tiny seconds, all equally tepid, each one like the other, but swift, but swift. Heaven knew what they still intended to do. That *he* should be the one whom this befell, he who felt every sort of draught as an insult! Now he would sit there, and the current would go past him like this, ceaselessly, his whole life long. He foresaw all the attacks of neuralgia that would result; he was beside himself with rage. He leaped up; but his surprises were not yet at an end. Beneath his feet as well, there was a kind of motion, not one movement only, but several, intermingling in a curious oscillation. He went stiff with terror. Could that be the earth? Certainly it was the earth. And the earth moved after all. He had heard about that at school; but it was passed over rapidly and gladly hushed up afterwards; it was not fitting to speak of it. But now that he had become sensitive, he was able to perceive this, too. Did others feel it? Perhaps, but they did not show it. Probably it did not bother them, these sailor-folk. But Nikolai Kusmitch was unquestionably rather delicate in this respect; he avoided even the street-cars. He staggered about in his room as if he were on the deck of a ship, and had to support himself right and left. To his further misfortune he remembered vaguely something about the oblique position of the earth's axis. No, he could not stand all these movements. He felt sick. Lie down and keep quiet, he had once read somewhere. And since that time Nikolai Kusmitch had been lying.

He lay and kept his eyes closed. And there were periods, days of easier motion, so to speak, when life was quite tolerable. And then he had thought out this expedient of the poems. One would scarcely have believed how it helped. When one recited a poem slowly, with even accentuation of the rhymes, one had, to a certain extent, something stable on which to keep a steady gaze, inwardly, of course. How fortunate that he knew all these poems by heart! But he had always been specially interested in literature. He did not complain about his state, the student who had known him for a long time assured me. Only in course of time an exaggerated admiration had grown in him for those who, like the student, could go about and bear the motion of the earth.

I remember this story so accurately because it greatly reassured me. I may well say I have never again had such an agreeable neighbour as this Nikolai Kusmitch, who surely would also have admired even me.

*

AFTER this experience I resolved in similar cases to go at once straight to the facts. I perceived how simple and reassuring they were compared with conjectures. As if I did not know that all our inferences are only supplementary; they are a winding up of accounts, nothing more! Immediately a new page begins, with an entirely different account, nothing carried forward. Of what help in the present case were the few facts, which it was child's play to establish? I shall relate them immediately, when I have told what concerns me at the moment: that these facts tended rather to aggravate the situation, which (as I now admit) was really difficult.

Let it be said to my honour, that I wrote a great deal in these days; I wrote with convulsive ardour. When I went out, it is true, I did not look forward to coming home again. I even made short detours and in this way lost a half-hour during which I might have been writing. I admit that this was a weakness. Once in my room, however, there was nothing with which I could reproach myself. I wrote: I had my own life, and the life next door to me was quite another life, in which I had no part: the life of a medical student, who was studying for his examination. I had nothing of a similar nature in prospect; that already constituted a decisive difference. And in other respects as well our circumstances were as different as could be. That was all clear to me. Until the moment, when I knew that *it* would come; then I forgot that there was nothing in common between us. I listened so intently that my heart beat loudly. I left everything and listened. And then it came: I was never mistaken.

Almost everyone knows the noise made by any round, tin object, such as the lid of a canister, when it slips from one's grasp. As a rule it does not make a loud noise when it reaches the floor; it falls sharply, rolls along on its edge, and really becomes disagreeable only when its momentum runs down and it bumps, wobbling in every direction before it comes to rest. Now, that is the whole story: a tin object of the kind fell in the next room, rolled, lay still, and, as this took place, stamping could be heard at certain intervals. Like all noises that impress themselves by repetition, this also had its internal organisation; it ran its course, never exactly the same. But it was that fact precisely which guaranteed its lawfulness. It could be violent or mild or melancholy; it could pass precipitately, as it were, or glide unendingly long before it came to rest. And the final oscillation was always surprising. On the other hand, the stamping that accompanied it seemed almost mechanical. But it punctuated the noise each time in a different manner; that seemed to be its function. I can now review these details much more accurately; the room next mine is empty. The student has gone home, somewhere in the country.

He needed to recuperate. I live on the top storey. On my right is another house; no one has moved into the room under me; I am without neighbours.

In this situation I am almost astonished that I did not take the matter more lightly. Although I was warned in advance every time by my senses. I should have profited by that. 'Don't be afraid!' I ought to have said to myself, 'It is coming now.' For I knew I was never deceived. But my emotion was perhaps due to the very facts with which I had acquainted myself; after I knew them I was still more liable to be terrified. There was something almost ghostly in the effect produced on me by the thought that this noise was caused by that small, slow, soundless movement with which the student's eyelid automatically sank and closed over his right eye, while he read. This was the essential thing in his story, a mere trifle. He had already allowed his examinations to lapse a few times; he had become sensitive in his ambition; and probably his people at home brought pressure to bear on him whenever they wrote. So what remained but to make a last attempt? But several months before the decisive date, this weakness had supervened, this slight, impossible fatigue, that seemed so foolish, as when a window-blind refuses to stay up. I am sure that for weeks he felt he ought to be able to master it. Otherwise I should never have thought of offering him my own will. For one day I knew that he had come to the end of his will-power. And, after that, whenever I felt the thing coming, I stood on my side of the wall and begged him to make use of mine. And in time it became clear to me that he was accepting it. Perhaps he ought not to have done so, especially when one reflects that it did not help. Even supposing we managed to achieve a slight delay, it is still questionable whether he was actually in a position to make use of the moments we thus gained. And meantime the outlays I had to make were beginning to tell on me. I know that I was wondering whether things could go on much longer in this fashion, on the very afternoon that someone came up to our floor. The staircase being narrow, this always caused considerable disturbance in our small hotel. After a little it seemed to me that someone entered my neighbour's room. Our two doors were the last in the passage, his being at an angle to mine and close to it. But I knew that his friends visited him occasionally, and, as I have said, I took absolutely no interest in his affairs. It is possible that his door was opened several times more, that there was coming and going outside. For that I really was not responsible.

Only on this same evening it was worse than ever. It was not yet late, but being tired I had already gone to bed; I thought I should probably go to sleep. Suddenly I sprang up as if someone had touched me. Immediately after, it began. It leaped and rolled and bumped against something, swaying and clattering. The stamping was frightful. In the intervals someone on the floor below knocked distinctly and angrily against the ceiling. The new lodger, too, was naturally disturbed. Now: that must be his door! I was so wide awake that I thought I heard his door open, although he was so astonishingly careful with it. It seemed to me he was approaching. He would certainly be wanting to know which room the noise was coming from. What alienated me was his really exaggerated consideration. He ought just to have noticed that quietness was a matter of no account in that house. Why in all the world did he step so softly? For a moment I thought he was at my door; and then I heard him — there was no doubt about it — entering the next room. He walked straight in.

And now (how shall I describe it?), now all was still. Still, as when some pain ceases. A peculiarly perceptible, prickling stillness, as if a wound were healing. I might have gone to sleep at once; might have taken a deep breath and gone off. My amazement alone kept me awake. Someone was speaking in the next room, but that, too, was part of the stillness. One must have experienced that stillness to know what it was like; it is impossible to describe. Outside, too, everything seemed to have been smoothed out. I sat up and listened; it was like being in the country. My God, I thought, his mother is there! She was sitting beside the lamp, talking to him; perhaps he had leaned his head a little against her shoulder. In a minute she would be putting him to bed. Now I understood the faint steps outside in the passage. Ah, that this could be! A being such as this, before whom doors yielded quite otherwise than they did for us! Yes, now we could sleep.

*

I HAVE almost forgotten my neighbour already. I fully realise that it was no real sympathy I had for him. Occasionally, indeed, I ask downstairs as I pass, what news, if any, there is of him. And I am glad when it is good news. But I exaggerate. In reality I do not need to know. It no longer has any connection with him if I sometimes sense a sudden impulse to enter the room next mine. It is but a step from my door to the other, and the room is not locked. It would interest me to know what the room is really like. It is easy to form an idea of any particular room, and often the idea corresponds quite closely to the reality. Only the room that is next door to one is always entirely different from what one imagines.

I tell myself that this is the thing which attracts me. But I know perfectly well that it is a certain tin object awaiting me there. I have assumed that some tin lid is really in question, though of course I may be mistaken. That does not trouble me. It accords with my present mental attitude to attribute everything to a tin lid. He was not likely, one thinks, to take it away with him. Probably the room has been cleaned and the lid put back on the tin where it belongs. And now both together form the concept 'tin,' a round tin, to express it exactly, a simple and very familiar concept. I seem to recall them standing on the mantel, these two parts that constitute the tin. Yes, they even stand before the mirror, so that another tin appears behind it, a deceptively similar, imaginary tin, a tin on which we place no value, but which a monkey, for example, would try to seize. In fact, there would even be two monkeys grabbing for it, for the monkey would also be duplicated when it approached the edge of the mantel-piece. Now then, it is the lid of this tin that had designs on me.

Let us agree on this matter. The lid of a tin, of a sound tin, whose edge is no more dented than its own — such a lid can have no other desire than to be upon the tin; this would be the utmost it could imagine for itself, an insurpassable satisfaction, the fulfilment of all its desires. Indeed, is there not something ideal in reposing evenly against the small projecting rim, after being patiently and softly turned to fit it, and feeling its penetrating edge within you, elastic, and just as sharp as your own edge is when you lie alone? But, alas, how few lids there are that can appreciate this! Here it is very evident what confusion has been wrought among things by their association with people. For human beings — if it be permitted to compare them just in passing with such tin lids — fit their occupations most badly and with no good grace. Partly because in their haste they have not found the right ones, partly because they have been placed on them awry and in anger, partly because the corresponding edges have been distorted, each in a different way. Let us be honest: their chief thought is, as soon as they get a chance, to jump down and roll around and make a tinny noise. Whence, otherwise, come all these so-called amusements and the noise they cause?

Things have watched this spectacle for centuries now. No wonder they are spoiled, no wonder they lose their taste for their natural, silent functions and want to make the most of existence, as they see it being done round about them. They try to shun their duties; they grow listless and negligent, and people are not surprised when they catch them red-handed in some disorderly action. They know so well from their own experience. They are annoyed because they are the stronger, because they think they have more right to change, because they feel they are being aped; but they let the matter go, as they let themselves go. But wherever there is one who gathers his forces together, some solitary, for example, who wants to rest roundly on his whole circumference, day and night, he straightway provokes the opposition, the contempt, the hatred of those degenerate objects which, with their bad consciences, cannot endure that anything should control itself and strive for significance. Then they combine to trouble, frighten and mislead him, and know they can do it. Winking to one another, they set about their conspiracy of seduction, which then grows beyond all measure, and sweeps into itself all creatures, and God Himself, against the solitary one who, perhaps, will triumph over it: the saint.

*

How well I understand now those strange pictures in which things meant for restricted and regular uses distend and wantonly touch and tempt one another in their curiosity, quivering with the casual lechery of dissipation: cauldrons that go about boiling over pistons that have ideas, useless funnels that squeeze themselves into holes for their pleasure! And behold! among them, too, thrown up by the jealous void, members and limbs, and mouths pouring their warm vomit into them, and windy buttocks, offering them satisfaction.

And the saint writhes, and shrinks into himself; yet there was a look in his eyes that admitted the possibility of these things: he glanced at them. And already his senses are forming a precipitate in the clear ichor of his spirit. Already his prayer is stripped of its foliage and stands up out of his mouth like a wilted shrub. His heart is overturned and has flowed out into the surrounding turbidity. His scourge falls as weakly upon him as a tail that flicks off flies. His sex is once again in one place only and when a woman comes straight through the huddle towards him, her naked bosom full with breasts, it points towards her like a finger.

There was a time when I thought these pictures obsolete. Not that I doubted their reality. I could imagine that this might have happened to saints long ago, those zealous pioneers, who wanted to be with God immediately at any cost. We no longer have the courage for this today. We suspect that God is too difficult for us, that we must defer Him, in order slowly to accomplish the protracted toil that separates us from Him. But now I know that this toil is just as much fought over as saintliness; that this struggle confronts everyone who for the sake of that labour is alone, as it faced the hermits of God in their caves and bare retreats, long ago.

*

WHEN we speak of hermits, we take too much for granted. We imagine that people know something about them. No, they do not. They have never seen a solitary; they have simply hated him without knowing him. They have been his neighbours who made use of him; they have been the voices in an adjoining room that tempted him. They have incited things against him, that they made a great noise and drowned his voice. Children have been in league against him because he was tender and a child, and as he grew, the stronger grew his opposition to grown people. They tracked him to his hiding place, like a hunted beast, and his long youth had no closed season. And when he did not sink exhausted, but escaped, they decried what had come forth from him, and called it ugly and cast suspicion upon it. And, when he paid no heed, they came out into the open and ate away his food, breathed his air and spat upon his poverty so that it became repugnant to him. They denounced him, as one stricken with contagious disease, and cast stones at him to make him depart more quickly. And they were right in their ancient instinct: for he was in truth their foe.

But, then, when he never raised his eyes, they began to reflect. They suspected that with all this they had simply done what he desired, that they had been fortifying him in his solitude and helping him to cut himself off from them for ever. And now they changed their tactics, and used against him the final weapon, the deadliest of all, the opposite mode of attack — fame. And at this noise he has almost every time looked up and been distraught.

*

Tonight there has come to my mind once more the little green book which I must have once possessed when I was a child, and I do not know why I imagine it came from Mathilde Brahe. It did not interest me when I got it, and it was not until several years later, I believe, during my holidays at Ulsgaard, that I read it. But important it was to me from the very first moment. It was charged with meaning through and through, even externally considered. The green of its binding meant something, and one saw at once that its contents would be what they were. As if by pre-arrangement, there came first that smooth fly-leaf, watered-white on white, and then the title-page which had an air of mystery. It looked as if there might well have been illustrations in it; but there were none, and one had to admit, almost reluctantly, that this, too, was just as it ought to be. There was some little compensation for this disappointment in finding, at a particular passage, a narrow book-mark, which, friable and a little awry, pathetic in its confidence that it was still rose-coloured, had lain since Heaven knows when between the same two pages. Perhaps it had never been used, and the book-binder had carefully and busily bound it in without looking at it closely. But possibly its position was not accidental. It may be that someone ceased reading at that point, who never read again; that fate at that moment knocked at his door so to engage him that he came far from all books, which after all are not life. It was impossible to tell whether the book had been read further. But it might also have been simply that the book had been opened and read again and again at this passage, and that this reading had taken place often, even if sometimes not until late at night. In any case I felt a certain shyness before those two pages, such as one feels before a mirror in front of which someone is standing. I never read them. I do not even know whether I read the whole book through. It was not very large, but there were a great number of stories in it; especially of an afternoon, when there was always one you had not yet read.

I remember only two of them. I will tell which they were: The End of Grishka Otrepioff, and The Downfall of Charles the Bold.

God knows whether it impressed me at the time; but now, after so many years, I recall the description of how the corpse of the false czar had been thrown among the crowd and lay there three days, stabbed and mangled, with a mask on its face. There is, of course, not the least prospect that the little book will ever come into my hands again. But this passage must have been remarkable. I should also like to read over again how the encounter with his mother took place.

He must have felt very sure of himself, since he commanded her to come to Moscow. I am even convinced that his belief in himself was so strong at that period, that he really thought he was summoning his mother. And this Maria Nagoi, who arrived from her mean convent by rapid day journeys, had, after all, everything to gain by assenting. But did not his uncertainty begin when she acknowledged him? I am not disinclined to believe that the strength of his transformation consisted in his no longer being the son of anyone in particular.

(This, in the end, is the strength of all young people who have gone away.) *

The fact that the nation desired him, having no idea of what a czar was like, only made him freer and more unbounded in the exercise of his powers. But the mother's declaration, even though it was a conscious deception, had still the power to belittle him; it curtailed the wealth of his inventiveness; it limited him to weary imitation; it reduced him to an individual other than himself; it made him an impostor. And now there also came, more gently dissolvent, that Marina Mniczek, who in her own fashion denied him, since, as it afterwards appeared, she believed not in him but in everyone. Naturally, I cannot be sure how far all this was considered in that story. It seems to me it should have been told.

But that aside even, this incident is not at all out of date. One might even now conceive of a writer, who would devote much care to these last moments;

* Written on the margin of the MS.

he would not be wrong. They are crowded with incident: how, waking from the deepest sleep, he leaps to the window, and through it into the courtyard between the sentinels. He cannot get up alone; they have to help him. Probably he has broken his leg. Leaning on the two men, he feels that they believe in him. He looks round: the others too believe in him. He is almost sorry for them, these gigantic Strelitzers; things must have come to a pretty pass with them: they have known Ivan Grosny in all his reality, and they believe in him. He is almost tempted to enlighten them; but to open his lips would simply mean to scream. The pain shoots maddeningly through his leg, and he has so little pride at the moment, that he is conscious of nothing but the pain. And then there is no time. They are crowding in: he sees Shuisky, and behind him all the others. Soon it will all be over. But now his guards close round him. They do not give him up. And a miracle happens. The faith of these old men spreads; suddenly, not a soul will advance. Shuisky, close beside him, calls up in desperation to a window above. The false czar does not look round. He knows who is standing there; he realises that there is silence, sudden silence. Now the voice will come that he knows of old, the shrill, false voice that overstrains itself. And then he hears the czarina, his mother, disowning him.

Up to this point the whole incident moves of itself; but now, pray, a narrator, a narrator! For from the few lines of the story that still remain to be written, there must emerge a force that shall transcend every contradiction. Whether it is so stated or not, one is ready to swear that between voice and pistol-shot, infinitely close, there was once again within him the will and the power to be everything. Otherwise one fails to understand how magnificently logical it was that they should pierce through his night-dress and stab him all over, as if to reach the hard core of a personality. And that in death, he should still have worn, for three days, the mask which already he had almost renounced.

*

When I consider the matter now, it seems strange to me that in the same book there should be an account of the end of a man who remained all his life long one and the same, a man hard and unchangeable as granite, who weighed ever more heavily on those who had to endure him. There is a portrait of him in Dijon. But even without that we know that he was squat, broad-backed, defiant, and desperate. Only his hands, perhaps, we should not have expected. They are excessively warm hands, that continually want to cool themselves and involuntarily lay themselves on any cold object, outspread, with air between the fingers. The blood could shoot into those hands, as it mounts to a person's head; and indeed, when clenched, they were like the heads of madmen, raging with fantasies.

It required incredible caution to live in peace with this blood. The duke was imprisoned with it in himself, and at times he was afraid of it, when it moved round in him, cringing and dark. Even to him it could appear

terribly foreign, this agile, half-Portuguese blood he
scarcely knew. He was often in terror lest it should
attack him as he slept and rend him in pieces. He
pretended to master it, but he lived always in the
shadow of his fear. He never dared to love a woman
lest it should be jealous, and so fiery was it that wine
never passed his lips; instead of drinking, he cooled
it down with a preparation of roses. Yet once he drank,
in the camp at Lausanne, when Granson was lost. He
was ill then and abandoned and he took much un-
diluted wine. But his blood had been sleeping then.
During his senseless last years it sometimes fell into
this heavy, bestial sleep. Then it appeared how com-
pletely he was in its power; for when his blood slept
he was nothing. On these occasions none of his en-
tourage was allowed to enter his presence; he did not
understand what they said. To the foreign envoys he
could not show himself, dejected as he was. Then he
sat and waited until his blood should awake. And
most often it would leap up suddenly and break out of
his heart and roar.

For the sake of this blood he dragged about with
him all those things on which he set so little store.
The three great diamonds and all the other precious
stones; the Flemish laces, and the Arras tapestries, in
piles. His silken pavilion with its cords of twisted gold,
and the four hundred tents for his suite. And pictures
painted on wood, and the twelve Apostles in massive
silver. And the Prince of Taranto, and the Duke of
Cleves, and Philip of Baden, and the seigneur of
Château-Guyon. For he wanted to persuade his blood

that he was emperor and nothing was above him, so that it might fear him. But his blood did not believe him, despite these proofs; it was such distrustful blood. Perhaps he kept it for a little time in doubt. But the horns of Uri betrayed him. After that his blood knew it inhabited a lost man; and it wanted to escape.

That is how I see it now; but at that time what used to impress me above all was to read of their search for him on the day of the Epiphany.

The young Lothringian prince, who had ridden the day before into his miserable town of Nancy, after that remarkably precipitate battle, had awakened his entourage very early and asked for the duke. Messenger after messenger was dispatched, and he himself appeared at the window, from time to time, restless and anxious. He did not always recognise those whom they carried in on their carts and litters; he only saw that none of them was the duke. Nor was he among the wounded, and none of the prisoners, whom they were continually bringing in, had seen him. But the fugitives carried discrepant accounts in every direction, and were confused and terrified, as though they feared to run upon him in their flight. Night had already begun to fall and nothing had been heard of him. The news that he had disappeared had time to get about during the long winter evening. And, wherever it came, it produced in everybody a brusque, exaggerated certainty that he lived. Never before, perhaps, was the duke so real to the imagination of all as on that night. There was no house where people did not keep watch and expect him and imagine that they heard him knocking. And if he did not come, it was because he had already gone by.

It froze that night, and it was as though the idea that he still existed had frozen as well, so solid was it. And years and years passed before it dissolved. All these people, without really knowing it, depended on his being alive. The destiny which he had brought upon them was tolerable only through his presence. It had been so hard for them to learn that he existed; but now, knowing him, they found him good to remember and not to be forgotten.

But next morning, the seventh of January, a Tuesday, the search for him was nevertheless resumed. And this time there was a guide. He was one of the duke's pages, and it was said that he had seen from a distance where his master fell; now he was to show the spot. He himself had told nothing; Count Campobasso had brought him and had spoken for him. Now he walked in front, the others keeping close behind him. Who ever saw him so, muffled in a bizarre costume and strangely uncertain, would have found it difficult to believe this really was Gian-Battista Colonna, who was beautiful as a young girl and slender of limb. He shivered with cold; the air was stiff with the night-frost, the snow crunched under foot like the gnashing of teeth. They were all cold, for that matter. The duke's fool, nicknamed Louis-Onze, kept himself constantly in motion. He imitated a dog, ran ahead, came back, and trotted for a little on all fours beside the boy; but whenever he saw a corpse in the distance he leaped towards it and bent over it and urged it to pull itself together and be the one they were seeking. He gave it a little time for reflection, but then came back grumbling to the others and threatened and swore, and complained of the sloth and the obstinacy of the dead. And they went on and on, without end. The town could scarcely be seen now; for the weather had become lowering, in spite of the cold, and the sky was grey and impenetrable. The country lay there flat and indifferent, and the little compact group looked more and more lost, the further it moved on. No one spoke; only an old woman, who had been running behind them, mumbled something and shook her head: perhaps she was praying.

Suddenly the leader of the little band stood still and looked about him. Then he turned to Lupi, the duke's Portuguese doctor, and pointed to something ahead. A few steps further on there was a stretch of ice, a kind of pond or marsh, and in it there lay, half-immersed, ten or twelve dead bodies. They were almost completely stripped and despoiled. Lupi, bowed and attentive, went from one to the other. And as they went thus separately about among the bodies, they recognised Olivier de la Marche and the chaplain. But the old woman was already kneeling in the snow and whimpered as she bent over a large hand, whose out-spread fingers pointed stiffly towards her. They all ran forward. Lupi, with some of the attendants, tried to turn over the body, which was lying on its face. But the face was frozen into the ice, and as they pulled it out, one of the cheeks peeled off, thin and brittle, and it appeared that the other cheek had been torn out by dogs or wolves, while a large wound cleft the whole from ear to ear, so that it could not be called a face at all.

Each one looked round in turn; each expected to find the Roman behind him. But they saw only the fool; who came running towards them angry and bleeding. He held a cloak away from him, and shook it as if something should fall out of it; but the cloak was empty. Then they began to look for marks by which to identify the duke, and they found a few. A fire had been kindled and the body was washed with warm water and wine. The scar on the throat appeared, and the traces of the two large abscesses. The doctor no longer had any doubt. But still further evidence was found. Louis-Onze had discovered, a few steps away, the dead body of the big black charger Moreau, whom the duke had ridden at the battle of Nancy. He was sitting astride it, letting his short legs hang down. The blood was still running from his nose into his mouth, and one could see him tasting it. One of the attendants standing on the other side remembered that the duke had had an ingrown nail on his left foot, and now they all began to search for this nail. But the fool wriggled, as if he were being tickled and cried, 'Ah! Monseigneur, forgive them for revealing your gross defects, dolts that they are, and not recognising you in my long face, in which your virtues are written!'

(The duke's fool was also the first to enter the room where the corpse was laid out. It was in the house of a certain Georges Marquis, no one could say for what reason. The winding-sheet had not yet been spread over the body, so the fool received the full impression. The white of the shroud and the crimson of the cloak stood in harsh, unfriendly contrast to each other between the two blacks of baldachin and couch. The scarlet long-boots stood in front, pointing towards him with their great, gilded spurs. And that that thing up there was a head there could be no dispute, as soon as one saw the coronet. It was a large, ducal coronet set with jewels of some sort. Louis-Onze moved about, inspecting everything carefully. He handled even the satin, though he knew little about it. It would be good satin, perhaps a trifle cheap for the house of Burgundy. He stepped back once more to survey the whole. The colours were singularly ill-assorted in the light reflected from the snow. He stamped each one separately on his memory. 'Well-dressed,' he acknowledged finally, 'perhaps a trifle too conspicuously.' Death seemed to him like a puppet-master in instant need of a duke.) *

*

IT is well simply to recognise certain things which will never alter, without deploring the facts or even judging them. Thus it became clear to me that I never was a real reader. In my childhood I considered reading a profession on which one would embark at some future time, when all the professions came up for consideration in turn. I had, to tell the truth, no

* Written on the margin of the MS.

clear idea when that might be. I trusted to the fact that one would notice when life somehow turned around and came only from without, as hitherto from within. I imagined that it would then become intelligible and unambiguous and not at all liable to misunderstanding; not simple, by any means — on the contrary, quite exacting, complicated, and difficult, if you like — but always visible. The child's strange feeling of the unlimited, the unconditional, of something never-really-to-be-foreseen, would then be surmounted; though indeed one did not at all know how. In reality that feeling still continued to grow, closing in on one from all sides; and the more one looked out on external things, the more did one stir up the things that were deep within: God knows whence they came! But probably they grew to a maximum and then suddenly broke off. It was easy to see that grown people were very little troubled by them: they went about, judging and doing, and if ever they got into difficulties, they blamed external circumstances.

Until the beginning of these changes, too, I postponed reading. One would then treat books as one treated friends, there would be time for them, a definite time that would pass regularly and agreeably, just so much of it as suited one. Naturally some of them would be closer to one than others, and this is not to say that one would be safe from wasting half-an-hour over them, now and again, to the neglect of a walk, an appointment, the first act of a play, or a pressing letter. But that one's hair should become untidy and dishevelled, as if one had been lying on it, that one should get burning ears and hands as cold as metal, that a long candle beside one should burn right down to its socket — these things, thank God, would be entirely out of the question!

I mention such occurrences because I myself experienced them, somewhat vividly, during those holidays at Ulsgaard, when I so suddenly took to reading. It became clear at once that I could not read. I had indeed begun my reading before the period I had in prospect assigned to it. But the year I spent at Sorö among so many others of about my own age had made me mistrustful of such reckonings. There some sudden and unexpected experiences had overtaken me; and it became plain that they dealt with me as if I were grown up. They were life-sized experiences that bore on me with all their weight. In the same degree, however, as I apprehended their actuality, my eyes opened also to the unending reality of my childhood. I knew that it would not cease, just as the other stage was only now beginning. I said to myself that everyone was naturally at liberty to draw lines of demarcation between the two, but they were hypothetical. And it appeared that I was not clever enough to think out any for myself. Every time I tried, life gave me to understand that it knew nothing of them. If, however, I persisted in thinking that my chilhood was past, then in that same moment my whole future also vanished and there was left me only just so much as a lead soldier has beneath his feet to stand on.

This discovery, as may well be understood, separated me still more from others. It busied me with myself and filled me with a kind of final joy, which I mistook for affliction, because it was far in advance of my age. I was disquieted also, as I recollect, by the fact that, since no definite period of reading had been planned beforehand, I might miss many things altogether. And when I returned to Ulsgaard in this state of mind and saw all the books, I set to in great haste, almost with a bad conscience. I had somehow a premonition of what I so often felt in after years: that one has no right to open a book at all, unless one is prepared to read them all. With every line one broke into the world. Before books came it was intact, and perhaps after reading them one would recover it entire again. But how could I, who was unable to read, cope with them all? There they stood, even in that modest library, in such hopeless abundance, so close together. I flung myself stubbornly and despairingly from book to book and rushed through their pages, like one who has to perform a task beyond his powers. At that time I read Schiller and Baggesen, Öhlenschläger and Schack-Staffeldt, all there was of Walter Scott and Calderon. Many things came into my hands which apparently I ought to have read before, while for others I was much too young; there was almost nothing suited to the stage I had reached then. And nevertheless I read.

In later years it occasionally happened that I awoke in the night, and the stars were so real and advanced so convincingly that I could not understand how people managed to lose so much of the world. I had a similar feeling, I believe, when I lifted my eyes from my books and looked outside, where summer was, where Abelone called me. It seemed very surprising to us that she had to call me and I did not even answer. That happened in the midst of our happiest time. But as the fever had now taken possession of me I clung convulsively to my reading, and hid, important and obstinate, from our daily holidays. Unskilled as I was in taking advantage of the numerous but often not too obvious opportunities of enjoying a natural happiness, I did not regret the promise our growing quarrel afforded of future reconciliations, which became the more delightful the longer they were postponed.

Furthermore, my reading trance ended as suddenly as it had begun; and then we thoroughly angered one another. For Abelone spared me no teasing or disdain, and when I met her in the arbour she would pretend to be reading. On a certain Sunday morning the book was indeed lying beside her unopened, but she seemed rather too busily employed over the currants, which with the aid of a fork she was carefully stripping from their little clusters.

It must have been one of those early mornings such as we have in July, fresh, rested hours, in which joyful and spontaneous things are happening everywhere. From a million tiny insuppressible movements a mosaic of most convincing life is created; objects vibrate one into another and out into the atmosphere, and their cool freshness makes the shadows vivid and gives the sunshine a light and spiritual clarity. In the garden no one thing stands out above the rest; everything is universally diffused, and one would have to be in all in order to lose nothing.

And in Abelone's slight gesture the whole was once again included. It was such a happy thought that she should be doing just that, and exactly as she did it. Her hands, lustrous in the shade, moved so lightly and harmoniously back and forth, and from the fork the round berries leaped playfully into the basin, in which fragrant vine-leaves had been laid, to join the others heaped up there, red and light gold, gleaming with points of light and enclosing sound grains within the acid pulp. In these circumstances I desired nothing save to look on; but, as I should probably be reproved for that, to keep myself in countenance I took the book, sat down on the other side of the table and, without long turning of pages, plunged into it at random.

'If only you would at least read aloud, bookworm,' said Abelone after a little. That did not sound nearly so quarrelsome, and, since I thought it high time for a reconciliation, I promptly read aloud, going right on to the end of a passage, and on again to the next heading: 'To Bettina.'

'No, not the answers,' Abelone interrupted, and suddenly laid down the little fork as if she were exhausted. Then she laughed at the look I gave her.

'Good heavens, Malte, how badly you read!'

Then I had to admit that not for one moment had I been thinking of what I was doing. 'I read simply to get you to interrupt me,' I confessed, and grew hot and turned back the pages till I came to the title of the book. Only then did I know what the book was. 'Why not the answers?' I asked with curiosity.

Abelone seemed not to have heard me. She sat there in her bright dress, as though she were growing altogether dark within, as her eyes were now.

'Give it to me,' she said suddenly, as if in anger, taking the book out of my hand and opening it at the page she wanted. And then she read one of Bettina's letters.

I do not know what I understood of it, but it was as though a solemn promise had been given me that one day I should grasp it all. And while her voice rose and at last almost resembled the voice I knew from her singing, I was ashamed that I had had so trivial a conception of our reconciliation. For I well knew that this was it. But it was taking place somewhere on a grand scale, far above me, in a region to which I could not attain.

*

THE promise is still being fulfilled. At some time that same volume appeared amongst my books, amongst the few books from which I shall never part. It opens, now, for me too, at the passages of which I am thinking, and when I read them I am uncertain whether it is Bettina or Abelone I have in mind. No, Bettina has become more real within me; Abelone, whom I knew, was like a preparation for her and has now been transmuted for me into Bettina, as if into her own unconscious being. For this, wonderful Bettina has by all her letters created space, a world of most spacious dimensions. From the beginning she diffused herself through the whole, as though she were already beyond her death. Everywhere she penetrated existence to its profoundest depths, as an integral part of it; and everything that happened to her was eternal in nature: in it she recognised herself, and she freed herself almost painfully, divined herself laboriously as if out of the past, evoked herself like a spirit, and confronted herself.

Just now you still existed, Bettina; I understand you. Is not the earth still warm with you? And do not the birds still make room for your voice? The dew is different, but the stars are still the stars of your nights. Or is not the whole world yours? For how often you have set it afire with your love, and watched it burn and blaze, replacing it in secret with another world, when all were asleep! You felt yourself entirely in accord with God, when every morning you sought a new world from Him, that all the worlds He had created might have their turn. You thought it unworthy to spare them or improve them and you used them as they were and stretched your hands out ever again for more. For your love had grown equal to everything.

How is it possible that all men do not still speak of your love? What has since happened that is more memorable? With what, then, are they occupied? You yourself knew the worth of your love; you uttered it aloud to your greatest poet, that he might make it human; for as yet it was but elemental. But he, in writing to you, dissuaded people from believing in it. They have all read his answers and believe them rather than your letters, because the poet is more intelligible to them than nature. But perhaps it will be shown some day that herein lay the limit of his greatness. This woman's love was forced upon him, and he could not gainsay it. What does it signify that he could not respond? Such love needs no response; it is itself the mating-call and the reply; it answers its own prayers. But the poet should have humbled himself before her in all his magnificence and written what she dictated, with both his hands, kneeling, like John on Patmos. There was no choice for him before this voice which 'fulfilled the angels' task,' which had come to wrap him round and bear him away into eternity. Here was the chariot of his fiery ascension. Here was prepared against his death the dark myth that he left uncompleted.

*

FATE loves to invent patterns and designs. Its difficulty lies in its complexity. But life is difficult because of its simplicity. It consists of a few things only, whose magnitude is not measurable by us. The saint, rejecting fate, chooses these as opposed to God. And because woman, following her nature, must make the same choice in regard to man, there is called forth the fatality inherent in all love-relationships. Resolute and above fate, like an eternal being, she stands beside him in his variability. The woman who loves always transcends the man she loves, because life is greater than fate. Her gift of herself she wants to make immeasurable; that is her happiness. And the nameless suffering of her love has always been this: that she is asked to limit her giving.

No other plaint have women ever raised. The two first letters of Heloïse contain that only, and five hundred years later it rises from the letters of the Portuguese nun; one recognises it as one does a bird-call. And suddenly through the clear field of this insight passes the very distant figure of Sappho, whom the centuries did not find because they sought her, not in life, but in fate.

*

I HAVE never dared buy a newspaper from him. I am not sure that he really carries any copies with him, as he shuffles slowly back and forth outside the Luxembourg Gardens, all evening long. He turns his back to the railings, and his hand rubs along the stone coping in which the bars are set. He presses himself so flat against it that every day many pass by who have never seen him. True, he possesses the remains of a voice that draws attention to his existence; but it is no louder than the noise in a lamp or a stove, or the odd, irregular dripping of water in a grotto. And the world is so arranged that there are people who, all their life long, pass by during the pauses, when he, more silent than anything else that stirs, moves on like the hand of a clock, like the shadow of that hand, like time itself.

How wrong it was of me to look at him reluctantly! I am ashamed to write down the fact that often when approaching him I adopted the tread of the others, as though I did not know he was there. Then I heard 'La Presse' spoken within him and immediately repeated and a third time, at hurried intervals. And the people beside me turned round and sought the voice. Only I made more haste than any of them, as though I had noticed nothing, as though I were inwardly and totally absorbed.

And indeed I was. I was occupied in picturing him to myself; I had undertaken the task of imagining him, and the exertion made the sweat break out on me. For I had to create him as one would a dead man, of whose existence there remain no proofs, no components; a dead man who has to be created entirely out of one's inner self. I know now that it helped me a little to think of those numerous diminutive Christs of striated ivory that lie about in every antiquary's shop. The thought of some *Pietà* came and went in my mind — no doubt simply to evoke the particular angle at which his long face was held, the pitiful aftergrowth of beard in the shadows of his cheeks, the unmistakable pain in the sealed-up aspect of his blind eyes that turned obliquely upwards. But there were so many other things besides that were part and parcel of him; for even then I knew nothing about him was unimportant: not the manner in which his coat or cloak, gaping at the back, let his collar be seen all the way round — that low collar, which curved in a wide arc round the stretched and hollow neck without touching it; not the greenish-black cravat wound loosely about the whole; and most particularly not the hat — an old, high-crowned, stiff felt hat which he wore as all blind men wear their hats, without regard to the lines of their faces, failing to form by this accession to their personality any new external unity, merely as an extraneous object taken for granted. In my cowardly refusal to look at this man I went so far that finally his image, often without cause, condensed with painful force in me to such sharp misery that, driven by it, I resolved to intimidate and suppress the increasingly precise picture in my imagination by confronting it with the external reality. It was towards evening. I decided to walk attentively past him at once.

Now you must know that spring was approaching. The wind of day had fallen; the side streets lay long and contented; where they debouched, the houses gleamed new and fresh, like recently broken fragments of some white metal, a metal that surprised one by its lightness. In the broad, smooth-flowing streets people thronged past one another, almost without fear of the vehicles, which were few. The tower-tops of Saint Sulpice stood out bright and unexpectedly high in the still air, and in the narrow, almost Roman alleys one had an unlooked-for glimpse into the season of the year. In the garden and before it there was such a mass of moving humanity that I did not see him at once. Or did I not recognise him at first among the crowd?

I knew at once that my conception of him was worthless. The utter abandonment of his misery, softened by no precaution or disguise, exceeded the powers of my imagination. I had grasped neither the angle of inclination in his attitude, nor the terror with which the inner side of his eyelids seemed constantly to fill him. I had never thought of his mouth, which was contracted like the opening of a gutter. Possibly he had memories, but now nothing found a way into his soul any more, save daily the amorphous feeling of the stone coping behind him on which his hand was gradually wearing itself away. I had stood still, and while I saw all this almost simultaneously, I felt that he was wearing another hat and a cravat that was undoubtedly meant for Sunday use only. It had a pattern of oblique yellow and violet checks, and as for the hat — it was a new cheap straw with a green band. These colours, of course, had no significance, and it is petty of me to have remembered them. Let me only say that on him they were like the softest down on a bird's breast. He himself got no pleasure from them, and who among all those people — I looked round about me — could imagine that all this finery was for him?

My God, it struck me with sudden vehemence, thus then art Thou! There are proofs of Thy existence. I have forgotten them all and have never demanded any, for what a formidable obligation would lie in the certainty of Thy existence! And yet it has just been proved to me. This, then, is to Thy liking, in this dost Thou take pleasure: that we should learn to endure all and not judge. What are the grievous things, and what the gracious? Thou alone knowest.

When winter comes again and I need a new cloak
— grant that I may wear it thus, so long as it is new!

*

Iᴛ is not that I want to distinguish myself from them,
when I go about in clothes that are better than theirs
and that have always belonged to me, and when
I insist on living in a definite place. It is simply that
I have not ventured so far as they: I have not the
courage to live their life. If my arm were to wither,
I believe I should hide it. But she (beyond this I do
not know who she was), she appeared every day in
front of the café terraces, and although it was very
difficult for her to take off her cloak and disentangle
herself from her confused garments and under-gar-
ments, she did not shrink from the trouble and took
so long divesting herself of one garment and another
that one could scarcely wait any longer. And then she
stood before us modestly, with her crooked, withered
stump, and one saw that it was something unusual.

No, it is not that I want to distinguish myself
from them. But I should think too much of myself
if I sought to be like them. I am not. I possess neither
their strength nor their capability. I take nourishment,
and from meal to meal I exist, and there is no secret
about it whatever; while they subsist almost like eter-
nal beings. They stand in their corners every day, even
in November, and winter does not make them cry out.
The fog comes and makes them indistinct and uncer-
tain: they exist notwithstanding. I went travelling,

I fell ill, many things happened to me: but they did not die.

(I do not even know how it is possible for school-children to get up in bedrooms filled with grey-smelling cold; who encourages them, those little, hurrying skeletons, to run out into the adult city, into the gloomy close of the night, into the everlasting school-day, still always puny, always full of foreboding, always too late. I have no conception of the amount of succour that is constantly being used up.) *

This city is full of people who are slowly gliding down to their level. Most of them resist at first; but then you have those pallid, ageing girls, who continually yield themselves without a struggle, strong, in their innermost being still unworn, but who have never been loved.

Dost Thou perhaps intend, O God, that I should leave everything and love them? Else why is it so difficult for me not to follow them when they overtake me? Why do I invent, of a sudden, the sweetest, most nocturnal words, and why does my voice linger softly in me between my throat and my heart? Why do I imagine how I would, with infinite precaution, hold them by my breath, these dolls with whom life has played, spring-time after spring-time, making them stretch out their arms for nothing, and again for nothing, until their shoulder-joints are loose? They have never fallen from any very high hope, so they are not shattered; but exhausted they are, and already life has no use for them. Only stray cats come to them in

* Written on the margin of the MS.

their rooms at evening and scratch them secretly, and lie sleeping on them. Sometimes I follow one of them the length of two streets. They walk along past the houses; people always come who screen them from view; they vanish away behind them into nothing.

And yet I know that if one tried to love them, they would weigh upon one, like those who have travelled too far and can walk no more. I believe that only Jesus could bear them, who still has resurrection in all His limbs; but they matter little to Him. It is only those who love that draw Him to them; not those who wait with a small talent for being loved, as with a lamp gone cold.

*

I KNOW that if I am destined for the worst it will avail me nothing to disguise myself in my best garments. Did he not slip down in the very midst of his royalty to take a place among the last of men — he, who instead of rising sank to the very bottom? It is true that at times I have believed in the other kings, albeit the parks no longer give proof of anything. But it is night; it is winter; I am freezing; I believe in him. For glory is but for a moment, and we have never seen anything more lasting than misery. But the king shall endure.

Is he not the only one who held up under his madness like wax flowers beneath a glass case? For the others they implored long life in their churches; but of him the Chancellor Jean Charlier Gerson demanded that he should be eternal, and this when he was already in his most pitiable estate, wretched and in sheer poverty despite his crown.

It was then when foreign-looking men with swarthy faces time and again fell upon him in his bed, to tear from him the shirt that had rotted in his ulcers, and that for a long while now he had taken for part of himself. It had grown dark in the room, and they ripped off the rotten rags, as they snatched them from under his rigid arms. One of them brought a light, and only then did they discover the purulent sore on his breast, into which the iron amulet had sunk because he pressed it to him every night with all the force of his ardour; now it lay deep in him, terribly precious, in a pearly froth of matter, like some miraculous relic in the hollow of a reliquary. The assistants had been chosen because they were hardened men, but they were not proof against disgust when the worms, disturbed, reached towards them out of the Flemish fustian and, falling from its folds, crept somewhere up their sleeves. His condition had undoubtedly grown worse since the days of the *parva regina*. For she had, at least, been willing to lie beside him, young and radiant as she was. Then she had died, and now no one had dared bed a sleeping companion beside that carrion. She had not left behind her the words and endearments with which the king was to be soothed. So none now penetrated the confusion of this spirit; none helped him out of the abysses of his soul; none understood, when he suddenly came out of them himself with the round-eyed gaze of an animal that goes to pasture. Then when he recognised the preoccupied countenance of Juvenal, he remembered the empire as it had been when last he knew it. And he wanted to retrieve what he had neglected.

But it was characteristic of the events of these times that they could not be cautiously described. Where anything happened, it happened with all its weight, and when spoken of it had to be told all of a piece. How could one have softened the fact that his brother had been assassinated; that yesterday Valentina Visconti, whom he always called his dear sister, had kneeled before him, lifting the voluminous black veil of her widowhood from her disfigured countenance, that was at once a lament and an accusation? And today a persistent and talkative advocate had stood there for hours demonstrating the right of the princely assassin, until the crime became transparent and as though it would rise in radiance to Heaven. And justice meant deciding in favour of all; for Valentina of Orleans died broken-hearted, although vengeance had been promised her. And of what avail was it to pardon and pardon again the Duke of Burgundy? Of him the sinister flame of his despair had taken possession, so that for weeks now he had been living in a tent deep in the forest of Argilly and declared that, for his solace, he must hear the stags belling in the night.

When all these things had been pondered, again and again from beginning to end, though no long time had elapsed, the people demanded to see their king, and they saw him — perplexed. But the people rejoiced at the sight. They realised that this was the king, this silent, patient man, who was there only that he might allow God to take action above him in His tardy impatience. In these lucid moments on the balcony of his palace at Saint-Pol, the king perhaps divined his own secret progress: he remembered the day of Roosbecke, when his uncle de Berry had taken him by the hand to lead him to the place of his first complete victory; there in the wonderful long light of that November day he had surveyed the masses of the men of Ghent, just as they stood, choked with their own dense formation when the cavalry had attacked them on every side. Intertwined with one another, like an immense brain, they lay there in the heaps they themselves had formed in order to present a compact front. Breath failed one at the sight of their suffocated faces; one could not help imagining that the air had been swept away far above these corpses, kept erect by their own pressure, through the sudden flight of so many despairing souls.

They had impressed this scene on the king's heart as the beginning of his glory. And he preserved the memory of it. But if that had been the triumph of death, this, as he stood here on his trembling legs, upright in the sight of all, this was the mystery of love. He had seen by the faces of others that that field of battle could be comprehended, immense though it was. But this which was happening now could not be understood; it was just as marvellous as, long ago, the stag with the collar of gold in the forest of Senlis. Only this time he himself was the apparition and others were lost in contemplation. And he doubted not that they were breathless, strung to the same high pitch of expectation that had overtaken him on that day in his youth at the chase, when the quiet face came peering at him from among the branches. The mystery of his being visible spread over all his gentle form; he did not stir for fear of vanishing; the slight smile on his broad, simple countenance took on a natural. permanence as in the faces of sculptured saints and was not strained. Thus he bore himself, and it was one of those moments that are eternity seen in foreshortening. The crowd could scarce endure it. Fortified, fed by an inexhaustible consolation, it broke the silence with a cry of joy. But above on the balcony there was only Juvenal des Ursins left, and into the next silence he cried that the king would come to the rue Saint-Denis, to the Brotherhood of the Passion, to witness the mysteries.

On such days the king was filled with a benign consciousness. Had a painter of that time been seeking a symbol of life in Paradise, he could have found no more fitting model than the tranquil figure of the king, as he stood at one of the high windows in the Louvre with drooping shoulders. He was turning the pages of the little book by Christine de Pisan, called 'The Way of the Long Apprenticeship,' and which was dedicated to him. He was not reading the erudite polemics of that allegorical parliament which had undertaken to discover the prince who should be worthy to rule over the whole earth. The book always opened afresh for him at the simplest passages; where it spoke of the heart which for thirteen long years, like a crucible over the fire of suffering, had only served to distil the water of bitterness for the eyes; he understood that true consolation only began when happiness had vanished long enough and was for ever gone. Nothing was more precious to him than this consolation. And while his gaze seemed to embrace the bridge beyond, he delighted to view the world through Christine's heart, lured into spacious ways by the great Cumæan, the world of those days: the adventurous seas, the strange-towered cities shut in by the pressure of wide-stretching deserts, the ecstatic loneliness of the assembled mountains, and the heavens, explored in fearful doubt, which closed only like an infant's skull.

But when anyone entered, the king took fright and his spirit slowly grew dull. He allowed them to lead him away from the window and give him something with which to occupy himself. They had accustomed him to spend hours over illustrations; and he was content with that. Only one thing annoyed him: that in turning the pages he could never keep several pictures in sight at the same time, and that they were fixed in their folios so that they could never be shifted about. Then someone remembered a game of cards that had been quite forgotten; and the king accorded his favour to him who brought it, so delighted was he with those gaily-coloured cartoons that were separable and easily handled and full of suggestion. And while card-playing became the fashion among the courtiers, the king sat in the library and played alone. Just as he now turned up two kings in succession, so God had recently placed him beside King Wenceslas; sometimes a queen died, then he laid an ace of hearts upon her that was like a gravestone. It did not astonish him that there were several popes in this game; he placed Rome yonder at the edge of the table, and here at his right hand was Avignon. He had no interest in Rome; for some reason or other he pictured it to himself as round and thought no more about it. But he knew Avignon. And hardly had he begun to think of it, when his memory recalled the lofty hermetic palace and overtaxed itself. He closed his eyes and had to take a deep breath. He feared bad dreams the following night.

On the whole, however, it was really a soothing occupation, and they were right in bringing him back to it again and again. Such hours confirmed him in his belief that he was the king, King Charles the Sixth. This is not to say that he exaggerated his own importance; he was far from considering himself anything more than one of these pieces of pasteboard; but the certitude grew within him that he too was a definite card, perhaps a bad one, played in anger, and always losing: but always the same card, never any other. And yet when a week had passed thus in the regular confirmation of his own existence, he would begin to feel a certain contraction within him. His skin grew tense across his forehead and on the back of his neck, as if he suddenly felt their contours too distinctly. No one knew the temptation to which he yielded then, when he asked about the mysteries and could hardly wait until they began. And when at last the time came, he lived more in rue Saint-Denis than in his palace at Saint-Pol.

The fatal thing about these acted poems was that they continually added to and extended themselves, growing to tens of thousands of verses, so that ultimately the time in them was the actual time; somewhat as if one were to make a globe on the scale of the earth. The concave stage, beneath which was hell and above which the level of Paradise was represented by a balcony of unrailed scaffolding fixed to a pillar, only helped to weaken the illusion. For this century had indeed made both heaven and hell terrestrial. It lived by the powers of both in order to survive itself.

These were the days of that Avignon Christendom, which had gathered round John the Twenty-second a generation earlier, when so many had fled thither instinctively for shelter, that at the place of his pontificate there arose, immediately after his accession, the mass of that palace, sealed and ponderous like a last refuge for the homeless souls of all. But he himself, the little, slight, unworldly old man, still lived openly. When, but just arrived, he at once began swift and daring action in every direction, dishes spiced with poison were already on his table; the contents of the first goblet had always to be poured out, for the piece of unicorn was discoloured when the cup-bearer drew it out. In his uncertainty, not knowing where to conceal them, this septuagenarian carried about the wax images which had been made of him that he might be destroyed in them; and he scratched himself on the long needles with which they had been stuck through. They might have been melted down; but these secret simulacra had filled him with such terror that, despite his strong will, he often feared that he might thereby deal himself a mortal blow and vanish like the wax in the flames. But the fear only made his shrunken frame drier and more enduring. And now the body of his empire was being threatened. At Granada the Jews had been incited to destroy all the Christians; and this time they had hired more terrible accomplices. No one, immediately after the first rumours, had any doubt concerning the conspiracy of the lepers; already several people had seen them throwing their horrible bundles of decomposing rags into the wells. It was not mere credulity that made people promptly believe this possible; faith, on the contrary, had become so heavy that it slipped from their trembling hands to the bottom of the wells. And once more the zealous old man had to avert poison from his blood. He had prescribed the Angelus for himself and his entourage, as a prophylactic against the demons of the twilight, at the time when he had given way to superstitious fancies; and now throughout the whole agitated world there sounded every evening the tones of that calming prayer. But with this exception all the bulls and letters he gave out were like spiced wine rather than a tisane. The empire had not trusted itself to his treatment; but he never tired of overwhelming it with evidences of its sickness, and already they were coming from the farthest East to consult this lordly physician.

But then the incredible happened. On All Saints'

Day he had preached at greater length and with more fervour than usual; seized by a sudden need, as though to see it again himself, he had exhibited his faith; had lifted it slowly and with all his strength out of its eighty-five-year-old tabernacle and displayed it in the pulpit. And immediately they had denounced him. All Europe cried out: this was an evil faith!

Then the pope disappeared. Day after day he did nothing; he remained on his knees in his oratory, and explored the secret of those who by taking action do injury to their souls. At length he reappeared, exhausted by his heavy meditations, and recanted. He recanted again and again. It became the passion of his senile spirit to recant. He would have the cardinals wakened at night in order to converse with them about his repentance. And perhaps what made his life last beyond the ordinary span was in the end simply the hope of humbling himself before Napoleon Orsini, too, who hated him and who refused to come.

James of Cahors had recanted. And it looked as if God Himself had wished to show him his error, when so soon after He brought about the advent of that son of the Duc de Ligny who seemed to await his coming-of-age on earth only that he might participate in spiritual delights with all the maturity of manhood. Many were alive who remembered this radiant youth in the days of his cardinalate, and recalled how on the threshold of his young manhood he had become a bishop and had died when scarcely eighteen in an ecstasy of consummation. The dead walked once again; for the air around his tomb, in which, set free, life lay in all its purity, wrought long upon the bodies of the dead. But was there not something of despair even in that too precocious sanctity? Was it not an injustice to all that the pure fabric of this soul should have been drawn through life only to dye it more brightly in the scarlet vat of that age? Did the world not feel something like a counter-blow when this young prince sprang away from the earth in his passionate ascension? Why did not these shining spirits abide among those who laboriously bore their candles? Was it not this darkness that had led John the Twenty-second to affirm that *before* the last judgment there could be no complete beatitude, not anywhere, even among the blessed? And indeed, how much stubborn tenacity was required to imagine that, while here on earth such dense confusion reigned, somewhere there were those who already basked in the light of God, leaning on His angels and assuaged by their inexhaustible vision of His face!

*

HERE I sit, on this cold night, writing, and I know all this. I know it, perhaps, because that man met me once when I was young. He was very tall; indeed, I believe his height must have been surprising.

Unlikely though it seems, I somehow managed to escape from the house alone, towards evening. I was running; I turned the corner of a street, and at the same instant I collided with him. I do not see how what happened then could take place within some five seconds. It will take much longer to relate the incident, however concise I may be. I had hurt myself in running against him; I was small, it seemed a good deal to me that I was not crying, and I was also involuntarily waiting to be comforted. As he did nothing, I took it that he was embarrassed; I supposed that he could not find the right pleasantry to relieve the situation. I was glad enough to help him; but in order to do so it was necessary to look him in the face. I have said that he was tall. Now he had not bent down to me as would have been natural, with the result that he stood at a height for which I was not prepared. There was still nothing before me but the scent and the peculiar roughness of his clothes which I had felt. Suddenly his face appeared. What was it like? I do not know, I do not wish to know. It was the face of a foe. And beside that face, close beside it, on the level of his terrible eyes, like a second head, was his fist. Ere I had time to lower my head, I was already running; I fled to his left and ran straight down an empty, horrible alley, an alley in a foreign town, in a town where nothing is forgiven.

It was then that I lived through what I now comprehend: that heavy, massive, desperate age. The age in which a kiss of reconciliation between two men was only a signal for the murderers who were standing near. These two drank from the same cup, they mounted the same steed before the eyes of all; it was even said that they would sleep in the same bed that night. And through all these contacts their aversion to one another became so strong that whenever one of them saw the pulsing arteries of the other, a sickening disgust rose within him as at the sight of a toad. The age in which brother attacked brother and held him prisoner because he had received the larger share of an inheritance. The king, indeed, intervened on behalf of the ill-used brother, and restored him his freedom and possessions; and the elder brother, occupied with adventures in other and distant lands, left him in peace and in his letters repented of his injustice. But the brother who had been released never recovered from all that had befallen him. The century shows him in pilgrim's habit going from church to church, inventing ever more extraordinary vows. Hung with amulets, he whispers his apprehensions to the monks of Saint Denis, and for long there stood inscribed in their registers the wax candle of a hundred pounds' weight which he thought good to dedicate to Saint Louis. He never had a life of his own; until the end he felt his brother's envy and anger like a grimacing constellation above him. And that Count de Foix, Gaston Phoebus, admired of all, had he not openly killed his cousin Ernault, the English king's captain, at Lourdes? But what was that manifest murder compared to his not having, as it so terribly chanced, put aside the sharp little pen-knife when, with that hand famed for its beauty, in quivering remorse he stroked the naked throat of his son as he lay before him? The room was dark; light had to be brought to see the blood, this blood that had come from so long a past and was departing now for ever from a noble race as it secretly issued from the tiny wound of this exhausted boy.

Who could be strong and refrain from murder? Who in that age did not know that the worst was inevitable? Here and there a man, whose eyes had during the day encountered the relishing glance of his murderer, would be overtaken by a strange presentiment. He would withdraw and shut himself up, write out his last will, and finally order the litter of osier twigs, the cowl of the Celestines, and the strewing of ashes. Foreign minstrels would appear before his castle, and he would give them princely rewards for their song, that was in harmony with his vague forebodings. There was doubt in the eyes of his dogs as they looked up at him, and they grew less and less sure of his commands. From the device that had served a whole life long, there quietly emerged a second meaning, new and clear. Many long-established customs appeared antiquated, but there seemed to be no substitutes for them being built up. If projects came up, one carried them out on a grand scale without really believing in them. On the other hand, certain memories came to assume an unexpected character of finality. Evenings, by the fire, one meant to abandon oneself to them; but the night outside, which one no longer knew, became suddenly very loud in one's hearing. One's ear, accustomed to so many nights both safe and perilous, distinguished the separate pieces of the silence. And yet it was different this time. It was not the night between yesterday and today: it was a night. Night! *Beau Sire Dieu,* and then the resurrection! Scarcely could verses in praise of some loved woman reach one in such hours. They were all disguised in aubades and *saluts d'amour,* and no longer recognisable under long, trailing, pompous names, at most to be but dimly guessed, as in the full, womanly, upward glance of a bastard son.

And then, before late supper there was that pensive consideration of the hands in the silver wash-basin. One's own hands. Could any coherence be brought into their activity, any sequence, any continuity in their grasping and relinquishing? No. All men attempted to be on both sides at once. They all neutralised one another: action there was none.

There was no action except on the part of the mission brothers. The king, when he had seen their gestures and their acting, devised the charter for them himself. He addressed them as 'his dear brothers'; never had anyone so affected him. Permission was accorded them in actual words to go about among the laity in the full significance of the characters they represented; for the king desired nothing more than that they should infect many with their ardour and sweep them into the current of their own vigorous and ordered action. For himself, he longed to learn from them. Did he not wear, just as they did, symbols and garments that had significance? When he watched them, he believed it must be possible to learn these things: how to come and go, how to speak out and turn away, so that there could be no doubt as to what one meant. Vast hopes flooded his heart. In this hall in the Hospital of the Trinity, so restlessly bright and so strangely indefinite, he sat every day in the best place, standing up in his excitement and concentrating his attention like a school-boy. Others wept; but he was inwardly filled with shining tears and only pressed his cold hands together in order to endure the scene. Occasionally at critical moments, when an actor who had done speaking stepped suddenly out of the range of his wide-opened eyes, the king lifted his face and was afraid: how long now had he been present, Monseigneur Saint Michael, up there near the edge of the platform, in his armour of silver shining like a mirror?

At such moments he rose. He looked about him as though meditating a decision. He was very near to understanding the counterpart of this acting here — the great, sinister, profane passion, in which he was taking part. But all at once this feeling was gone. They were all engaged in meaningless movements. Glaring torches advanced upon him, and formless shadows fell on the vaulting above. Men whom he did not know were dragging him about. He wanted to take part in the play; but nothing came from his lips, his movements resulted in no gestures. The people pressed so strangely round him, the idea came to him that he ought to have been carrying the cross. And he wanted to wait for them to bring it. But they were stronger than he, and they shoved him slowly out.

*

OUTWARDLY much has been changed. I know not how. But inwardly and before Thee, O my God, inwardly and before Thee, Who lookest on, are we not actionless? We discover, indeed, that we do not know our part; we look for a mirror; we want to rub off the paint, to remove all that is artificial and become real. But somewhere a bit of mummery that we forget still sticks to us. A trace of exaggeration remains in our eyebrows; we do not notice that the corners of our lips are twisted. And thus we go about, a laughing-stock, a mere half-thing: neither real beings nor actors.

*

It was in the theatre at Orange. Without really looking up, merely conscious of the rustic fragment that now marks its façade, I had entered by the attendant's little glass door. I found myself among prone columns and some small marsh-mallow shrubs; but they hid from me only for a moment the open shell of the auditorium with its ascending tiers of seats, which lay there, divided into sections by the afternoon shadows, like an enormous, concave sundial. I advanced quickly towards it. I felt, as I passed up through the rows of seats, how small I became in these surroundings. A little higher up a few visitors, unequally distributed, were standing about in idle curiosity; their attire was unpleasantly evident, but they seemed so small as to be scarcely worth noticing. For a while they looked at me, wondering at my littleness. That caused me to turn round.

Ah, I was completely unprepared! A play was on. An immense, a superhuman drama was in progress, the drama of that gigantic scenery, the vertical tripartite structure of which was now visible, resonant in its immensity, overwhelming almost, and suddenly measurable by sheer excess of size.

I yielded to a violent shock of pleasure. This which confronted me, with its shadows ordered in the semblance of a face, with the darkness concentrated in the mouth at the centre, bounded above by the symmetrically curled head-dress of the cornice: this was the mighty, all-disguising, antique mask, behind which the universe condensed into a face. Here, in this vast amphitheatre of seats, there reigned a waiting, empty, absorbent existence: all happening was yonder, gods and destiny; and thence (when one looked up high) came lightly, over the groining of the wall, the eternal procession of the heavens.

That hour, as I realise now, shut me for ever out of our theatres. What should I do there? What should I do before a stage on which this wall (the icon-screen of the Russian churches) has been demolished, because we no longer have the power to press the action, like a gas, through its hard mass, to come forth in full, heavy oil-drops? Today our plays fall in fragments through the coarse sieve of our stage, and collect in heaps and are swept away when there are enough of them. It is the same underdone reality that litters our streets and our houses, save that more collects there than can be coped with in one evening.

(Let us be honest about it, then; we do not possess a theatre, any more than we possess a God: for this, communion is needed. Every man has his own particular ideas and fears, and he allows others to see as much of them as is useful for him and as suits him. We continually spin out our faculty of understanding, that it may suffice us, instead of crying out to the icon-wall of our common misery, behind which the Inscrutable would have time to gather itself, and put forth all its strength.) *

*

HAD we a theatre, would you stand, O tragic one, again and again, so slight, so naked, so utterly without protective subterfuge, before those who satisfy their impatient curiosity with the spectacle of your grief? You, so unutterably touching, you foresaw the realisation of your suffering, when, acting that time in Verona, little more than a child, you held massed roses before you as a mask-like face which should the better hide you.

It is true you were an actor's child, and when your parents played they wanted to be seen. Your profession was to become for you what the nun's vocation was, without her suspecting it, for Marianna Alco-forado: a disguise thick and durable enough to let her suffer unrestrainedly behind it with the ardour with which invisible happy ones are blessed. In all the cities you visited they described your gestures; but they did not understand how, growing more hopeless from day to day, over and over again you held before you a poetic thought, that it might hide you. You held

* Written on the margin of the MS.

your hair, your hands, or any other opaque object, before the translucent passages. You dimmed with your breath those that were transparent; you made yourself small; you hid yourself as children hide themselves, and then you uttered that fleeting cry of happiness — surely an angel should have sought you then! But when you looked cautiously up, there was no doubt that they had seen you all the time, all those in that hateful, hollow space, filled with eyes: you, you, you, and nothing but you.

And you longed to hold your crooked arm towards them with the finger-sign that wards off the evil eye. You longed to snatch from them your face, on which they preyed. You longed to be yourself. Your fellow-actors lost courage; as if they had been caged with a pantheress, they crept along the wings and spoke what they had to, only not to anger you. But you drew them forward, and you posed them and dealt with them as if they were real things. The loose-hung doors, the deceptive curtains, the stage-fittings that had no reverse side, drove you to protest. You felt how your heart rose unceasingly towards an immense reality, and, afraid, you tried once more to detach their looks from you, as if they had been long gossamer threads.... But by that time they were already breaking into applause in their fear of the last extremity, as though at the last moment to ward off something that would constrain them to change their way of life.

*

A LIFE difficult and full of danger do those lead who are loved. Ah, that they might conquer themselves and become lovers! Around those who love is much security. No one suspects them any more, and they themselves are not in a position to betray themselves. In them the secret has grown consummate; they cry it out whole, like nightingales; they do not break it into bits. They make lament for one alone, but the whole of nature unites with them: it is the lament for an eternal being. They hurl themselves after the lost one, but already with their first steps they overtake him, and before them is only God. Their legend is that of Byblis, who pursued Caunus as far as Lycia. The urge of her heart drove her through many lands upon his track, and at last she came to the end of her strength; but so powerful was the impulse of her nature, that, sinking into the earth, she reappeared beyond death as a spring, hurrying, as a hurrying spring.

What else happened to the Portuguese maid, save that inwardly she became a spring? Or to thee, Heloïse? Or to all ye, ye lovers whose laments have come down to us — Gaspara Stampa, the Countess of Die, and Clara d'Anduze; Louise Labbé, Marceline Desbordes, Elisa Mercoeur? But poor, fleeing Aïssé, you hesitated and gave in. Weary Julie Lespinasse! Desolate legend of the happy pleasance, Marie-Anne de Clermont!

ı I still remember exactly how, one day long ago, at home, I found a jewel-casket. It was two hands-breadths large, fan-shaped, with an inlaid border of flowers on dark-green Morocco velvet. I opened it: it was empty. I can say this now after so many years. But at the time when I had opened it I saw only in what its emptiness consisted: in velvet, a little mound of light-coloured velvet, no longer fresh; in the groove where the jewel had lain, which, empty now but lighter by a trace of melancholy, disappeared into it. For an instant might this be endured. But with those who are backward in loving it is perhaps always thus.

*

TURN back the pages of your diaries. Was there not always a period about the time of spring when the bursting forth of the year struck you as a reproach? A longing to be glad was in you, and yet when you went out into the spacious open, a strangeness came into the air, and your step became uncertain as on a ship. The garden was beginning; but you — that was it — you dragged into it winter and the year that had passed; for you it was at best but a continuation. While you waited for your spirit to take part in the season, you suddenly felt the weight of your limbs; and something like the possibility of becoming ill crept into your sense of the future. You blamed your too light garments; you drew your shawl more closely round your shoulders; you ran right up the drive to the end, and then you stood with beating heart in the centre of the wide turn-around, determined to be at one with all these things. But a bird sang, solitary, and disowned you. Ah! did you have to die?

Perhaps. Perhaps the novelty consists in our surviving these — the year and love. Blossoms and fruit are ripe when they fall; animals are self-aware and find each other and are content. But we, who have projected God, can never finish. We postpone the satisfaction of our nature; we need still more time. What is a year to us? What are all the years? Ere yet we have begun with God, we are already praying to Him: let us survive this night! And then sickness! And then love!

That Clémence de Bourges should have had to die in her beginning! She who had not her peer; herself the loveliest among the instruments which she could play as none other could, unforgettable even in the least tones of her voice. So resolute was her maidenhood in its lofty purpose, that a lover in her overflowing passion could dedicate to this awakening heart a book of sonnets in which every verse was insatiate. Louise Labbé was not afraid of terrifying this child with the long sufferings of love. She revealed to her the nightly increase of desire; she promised her pain as a more spacious world; and she suspected that she herself, with her known sorrow, fell short of that which this adolescent soul darkly awaited and which made it beautiful.

*

GIRLS in my native land! May the loveliest of you on an afternoon in summer find in the dim library the little book that Jean de Tournes printed in 1556. May she take the cool, smooth volume out with her into the murmurous orchard, or to the phlox beyond, in whose over-luscious perfume hangs an essence of sheer sweetness. May she find it early. In the days when her eyes begin to take note of themselves, while her mouth is still young enough to fill itself with much too large pieces bitten from an apple.

And when the time for livelier friendships comes, may it be your secret to call one another Diké and Anactoria, Gyrinno and Atthis. May someone, a neighbour perhaps, an older man who has travelled much in his youth and has long been considered eccentric, reveal these names to you. May he invite you sometimes to his house, to taste his famous peaches or to inspect, up in the white corridor, his Ridinger engravings illustrating horsemanship, which are so much discussed that it is necessary to have seen them.

Perhaps you will persuade him to relate something of his past. Perhaps there is one among you who can induce him to bring out his old travel-diaries; who knows? The same, perhaps, who will one day succeed in making him disclose the fact that certain fragments of Sappho's poetry have come down to us, and who will not rest until she learns what is almost a secret, to wit, that this secluded man loved now and again to employ his leisure in the translation of these bits of verse. He has to admit that, for a long time now, he has not given his translations a thought, and what there is of them, he assures her, is not worth mentioning. Yet, he is glad now when these open-hearted friends of his press him to recite a strophe. He even rediscovers the Greek text in the depths of his memory, and recites it, because, according to him, the translation does not do it justice, and because he wants to show these young people the beautiful, pure substance of this gorgeous language, the massive structure of which has been wrought in so intense a flame.

All this warms him again to his work. Evenings of beauty, of youthfulness almost, return to him, autumn evenings, for example, that have long, peaceful nights before them. Then the light burns late in his study. He does not always remain bent over his pages; he often leans back and closes his eyes on a line he has read again and again, and its meaning passes into his blood. Never before has he been so certain of the ancient past. He could almost smile at the generations that have mourned it as a lost drama, in which they would have liked to play a part. Now he instantly understands the dynamic significance of that early world-unity, which was something like a new and simultaneous gathering up of all human labour. It does not trouble him that the resulting civilisation, almost totally made manifest, seemed to the gaze of many later ages to form a complete whole and a whole that had taken place as such. In those days the celestial half of life indeed really fitted on the cup-like shell of terrestrial existence, like two full hemispheres meeting to form a perfect orb of gold. Yet, scarcely had this occurred, when the spirits confined within it felt that this utter realisation was merely a symbol; the massive star lost weight, and rose into space, and on its golden sphere was distantly reflected the sadness of all that could not yet be conquered.

As he thinks thus, the recluse in his night, thinks and understands, he notices a plate with fruit lying on the window-seat. Involuntarily he takes from it an apple, and lays it before him on the table. How my life centres in this fruit! he thinks. Around all that is perfected arises and grows that which has still to be achieved.

And then, beyond the unachieved, there rises before him, almost too quickly, that slight figure straining towards the infinite which (according to Galien's testimony) they all meant when they said 'the poetess.' For as after Hercules' labours destruction and rebuilding of the world cried out to be fulfilled, so from the resources of existence all the ecstasies and despairs with which the ages must be satisfied pressed towards the deeds of her heart, in order that they might be lived.

Of a sudden he knows this resolute heart that was ready to carry through to the end the whole labour of love. He is not surprised that men misunderstood this heart; that in this lover, so far before her time, they saw only excess, not the new measure of united love and suffering. Nor that they had interpreted the legend of her life only as it would have been credible at that time; that finally, they had attributed to her the death of those whom the god incites, alone, to pour themselves out in a love without return. Perhaps even among the girl-lovers whom she moulded there were some who did not understand: how at the height of her activity she mourned not for any single man who had forsaken her embrace, but for that one, henceforth impossible, who had grown to the measure of her love.

Here the solitary thinker rises and goes to his window; his lofty room is too close to him; stars he would see, if that is possible. He has no delusions about himself. He knows that this emotion fills him because among the young girls of his neighbourhood there is the one with whom he is concerned. He has wishes (not for himself, no, but for her); on her account he understands, in a passing hour of the night, the exigency of love. He promises himself to tell her nothing of it. It seems to him the utmost he can do is to be alone and wakeful and on her account to think how right that great lover had been: when she knew that nothing is meant by the union of two beings save increased loneliness; when she broke through the temporal aim of sex with its infinite purpose; when in the darkness of embracing she strove not for satisfaction but for greater longing; when she disdained the thought that of two one must be the lover and one beloved, and bore those who were feeble in love to her couch, kindling them into lovers so that they left her. By such supreme farewells her heart became the heart of nature itself. Over-reaching fate, she sang the epithalamia of her latest lovers; extolled their nuptials; magnified the virtues of the coming bridegroom, that they might prepare themselves for him as for a god and surpass even his splendour.

*

ONCE more, Abelone, in recent years I felt you and understood you, unexpectedly, after I had long ceased to think of you.

It was at Venice, in the autumn, in one of those salons where passing foreigners gather round the lady of the house, who is as foreign as they are. These people stand about, tea-cup in hand, and are delighted whenever a well-informed fellow-guest turns them with a swift and cautious gesture towards the door, and whispers a name that sounds Venetian. They are prepared for the strangest names, nothing can surprise them; for, however limited their experience in other respects, in this city they abandon themselves nonchalantly to the most extravagant possibilities. In their customary existence they constantly confound the extraordinary with the forbidden, so that the expectation of something wonderful, which they now permit themselves, stamps their faces with an expression of coarse licentiousness. The feeling that at home only momentarily possesses them, at concerts, or alone with a novel, they openly express as a legitimate condition in these encouraging surroundings. Just as they let themselves, quite unprepared and unconscious of danger, be stimulated by the almost fatal avowals of music as by corporeal indiscretions, so without in the least mastering the secret of Venice they abandon themselves to the rewarding swoon of the gondola. Married couples no longer young, who during their whole tour have had only ill-natured rejoinders for one another, sink into silent accord; the husband is overcome with the pleasant weariness of his ideals, while she feels young again and nods encouragingly to the lazy natives, smiling as if she had teeth of sugar that were always melting. And if one listens, it appears that they are leaving tomorrow or the day after or at the end of the week.

So I stood among them and rejoiced that I was not going away. Soon it would be cold. The soft, narcotic Venice of their preconceptions and demands, disappears with those somnolent foreigners, and one morning the other Venice is there, the real Venice, awake, brittle to the breaking point, and not in the least dream-like: This Venice, willed into being in the midst of nothing and set on sunken forests, created by force, and in the end so thoroughly manifest. This hardened body, stripped to necessities, through which the sleepless arsenal drove the blood of its toil, and this body's penetrating spirit, ever spreading, more powerful than the perfume of aromatic lands. This inventive state, that bartered the salt and glass of its poverty for the treasures of the nations. This beautiful counterpoise of the world, which even in its embellishments is full of latent energies ever more finely ramified — this Venice!

The consciousness that I knew this city filled me amongst these deluded people with such a sense of opposition, that I looked up, wondering how I could unburden myself. Was it thinkable that in these rooms there was not one person who unconsciously awaited enlightenment upon the essential nature of his environment? Some young man, who would straightway understand that he was here being offered not merely enjoyment, but an example of a will more exacting and more severe than could be found elsewhere? I moved about; the truth within me made me restless.

Since it had laid hold of me here among so many people, it brought with it the desire to be expressed, defended, demonstrated. The grotesque notion seized me of demanding silence next moment by clapping my hands in hate against all their gabbled misunderstanding.

In this ridiculous mood I perceived her. She was standing alone in the dazzling light of a window, observing me, not precisely with her eyes, which were serious and thoughtful, but, one would have said, with her mouth, which ironically imitated the obviously irritated expression of my face. I felt at once the impatient tension in my features and assumed an indifferent look, whereupon her mouth resumed its natural, haughty expression. Then, after an instant's reflection, we smiled to each other simultaneously.

She reminded me, if you will, of a certain youthful portrait of the beautiful Benedicte von Qualen, who played a part in Baggesen's life. One could not look at the dark calm of her eyes without suspecting the clear darkness of her voice. Furthermore, the plaiting of her hair and the way her light dress was cut out at the neck were so reminiscent of Copenhagen, that I made up my mind to address her in Danish.

But I was not yet near enough to do so, when a stream of people pressed towards her from the other side of the room. Our exuberant countess, warm, enthusiastic and scatter-brained, accompanied by a number of her guests, pounced upon her intending to carry her off on the spot to sing. I was sure the young girl would excuse herself, on the ground that no one there could possibly be interested in listening to singing in Danish. And this she did, when they allowed her to reply at all. The throng round this radiant figure became more urgent. Someone knew that she also sang German. 'And Italian, too,' a laughing voice added with mischievous assurance. I knew of no excuse with which, in thought, I might have furnished her, but I did not doubt that she would hold out. An expression of dry mortification had already overspread the importuners' faces, tired with too prolonged smiling; the good countess, to preserve her importance, had already stepped back a pace, with an air of mingled pity and dignity — and then, when it was altogether unnecessary, she consented. I felt myself grow pale with disappointment; my gaze was heavy with reproach, but I turned away; there was no use letting her see that. She freed herself, however, from the others, and in an instant was by my side. Her dress shone upon me, the flowery perfume of her warmth enveloped me.

'I am really going to sing,' she said in Danish, close to my cheek, 'not because they wish it, nor for the sake of appearances, but because at this moment I must sing.'

Through her words broke the same irritated impatience from which she had just delivered me.

I slowly followed the group of people with whom she moved away. But near a high door I remained behind, allowing the others to move about and get themselves seated. I leaned against the black, mirroring surface of the door and waited. Someone asked what was going on, whether there was to be singing. I pretended I did not know. As I told the lie she had already begun to sing.

I could not see her. Gradually the circle round her cleared for one of those Italian songs foreigners consider very genuine because they are so manifestly conventional. She who sang it did not believe in it. She declaimed it laboriously; she made too great an effort. I knew when it finished by the applause that broke out in front. I was sad and ashamed. People began to move about, and I decided to join the first who should leave.

But all at once there was silence. It was a silence which just now no one would have thought possible; it lasted, it grew more tense, and now through it arose that voice. (Abelone, I thought, Abelone.) This time it was powerful, full and yet not heavy; of one piece, without a rent, without a seam. She sang an unknown German song. She sang it with singular simplicity like something inevitable. She sang:

'I do not tell thee of the nights I spend
In tears for thee, by sleep unblest,
For thee, in whose fair presence blend
Sweet weariness and cradled rest.
Thou does not breathe to me the thoughts that send
Slumber from thine eyes:
How should we then endure
The splendour and the torture
Of our burning sighs
If we refrained?'
          (A short pause, and then hesitatingly:)

'Ah! think how soon the lips that yield
Love's sworn confession, first unsealed,
 With lies are stained!'

Again the silence. God knows who made it. Then
the people stirred, jostled one another, apologised,
coughed. They were on the point of falling into a gen-
eral obliterating hubbub, when suddenly the voice
broke out, resolute, broad, intense:

'I am alone, but thou art here, in the multitude
 Of murmurs, and in fragrant airs, to share my
    solitude.
 In all thou hast a part.
 Alas! they vanished all, that ever lay in my em-
    brace;
 Thee have I never held, so thou dost stay, with re-
    born grace,
 For ever in my heart.'

No one had expected it. They all stood as if bowed
beneath that voice. And in the end her assurance was
so great that it seemed she had known for years that
at that moment she would have to sing.

*

I HAD sometimes wondered before that why Abelone
did not direct the fervour of her magnificent passion
towards God. I know that she longed to remove from
her love all that was transitive; but could her sin-

cere heart be deceived on that score? Did she not know that God is only a direction given to love, not its object? Did she not know she need fear no return from Him? Did she not recognise the restraint of this deliberate lover, who quietly defers desire so that we, slow as we are, may bring our whole heart into play? Or did she seek to avoid Christ? Did she fear to be held by Him half-way, to become His beloved? Was it for this reason she thought so unwillingly of Julie Reventlow?

I almost believe so, when I recall how lovers so simple as Mechthild, so passionate as Theresa of Avilla, so wounded as blessèd Rose of Lima, could sink back on this alleviation of God, compliant, yet beloved. Ah! He who was a succour for the weak does these strong souls a wrong: when they awaited nothing more but the endless road, once again, expectant at the gate of heaven, they meet a palpable form that spoils them with His welcome and troubles them with His virility. His heart's powerful lens assembles once again the already parallel rays of their hearts, and they whom the angels hoped to keep intact for God flame up and are consumed in the drought of their desire.

(To be loved means to be consumed. To love means to radiate with inexhaustible light. To be loved is to pass away, to love is to endure.)*

It is equally possible that Abelone attempted in later years to think with her heart, in order that she might come imperceptibly and directly into communion with God. I can imagine that letters from her

* Written on the margin of the MS.

exist which recall the attentive inward contemplation of Princess Amalie Galitzin; but if these letters were addressed to someone who for years had been near to her, how must he have suffered at her change! And she herself: I suspect she feared nothing so much as that spectral transformation which we do not notice because all its evidences are so alien to us that we constantly overlook them.

*

It will be difficult to persuade me that the story of the Prodigal Son is not the legend of one who did not want to be loved. When he was a child, everybody in the house loved him. He grew up knowing nothing else, and as a child he became accustomed to their tenderness.

But as a growing boy he sought to lay aside these habits. He could not put it into words, but when he wandered about outside the whole day and did not even want to take the dogs with him, it was because they too loved him; because he could read in their eyes obedience, expectancy, participation and solicitude; because even in their presence he could do nothing without pleasing or giving pain. But what he then desired was that inner indifference of spirit, which sometimes, of an early morning in the fields, seized him so unalloyed that he began to run, that he might have neither time nor breath to be more than a transient moment in which the morning becomes conscious of itself.

The secret of that life of his which never yet had been, spread out before him. Involuntarily he forsook the footpath and ran on across the fields, with arms outstretched as if by that breadth of reach he could make himself master of several directions at once. And then he would throw himself down behind some hedge, and no one cared what became of him. He peeled a willow-branch to make himself a flute, flung a stone at some little wild animal, leaned forward to make a beetle turn around: in all this there was no hint of fate, and the heavens passed over him as over the world of nature. At last came afternoon with all its suggestions. He was a buccaneer on the island of Tortuga, but he was not obliged to be that; he besieged Campêche, or took Vera Cruz by storm; he could be a whole army, or a general on horseback, or a ship on the ocean, according to his humour. But if it entered his head to kneel, then swiftly he became Deodatus of Gozon, and slew the dragon, and, hot with vexation, learned that this was the heroism of pride, not of obedience; for he spared himself nothing that was part of the game. But, however numerous his imaginary adventures might be, there was always time in between to be only a bird, if uncertain what kind. Only then came the return home.

Heavens, how much there was then to cast off and forget! For it was necessary to forget thoroughly; otherwise you betrayed yourself when they insisted on knowing. However you lingered and looked about, the gable of the house always appeared at last. The first window in the upper row kept its eye on you;

someone might be standing there. The dogs, who had been waiting with growing eagerness all day, rushed at you through the bushes, and drove you back into the person they believed you to be. And the house did the rest. Once you entered into its full odour, most things were already decided. Details might still be changed, but in the main you were the person for whom they took you there; the person for whom, out of his brief past and their own desires, they had long fashioned a life, the common life, which lay day and night under the influence of their love, between their hope and their suspicion, before their praise or their blame.

Useless for such a person to go upstairs with indescribable precaution. They will all be in the sitting-room, and if the door merely opens they will look in his direction. He remains in the dark; he will await their questioning. But then the worst happens. They take him by the hand and draw him towards the table; and all of them, as many as are present, gather inquisitively before the lamp. They have the best of it; they keep in the shadow, while on him alone falls, with the light, all the shame of having a face.

Shall he stay and pretend to live the sort of life they ascribe to him, and grow to resemble them in his whole appearance? Shall he divide himself between the delicate sincerity of his will and the gross deceit that spoils it even for him? Shall he give up the attempt to become something which might hurt those of his family whose spirits are but feeble?

No, he will go away. When, for example, they are all busy setting out on his birthday table those badly chosen gifts meant, once again, to compensate for everything. Go away for ever. Not until long afterwards is he to realise how firmly he had then resolved never to love, in order not to put anyone in the terrible position of being loved. Years later he remembers this, and, like other projects, this too became impossible. For he had loved and loved again in his solitude, each time with wasteful expenditure of his whole nature and with unspeakable fear for the liberty of the other. Slowly he learned to penetrate the beloved object with the rays of his passion, instead of consuming it in them. And he was spoiled by the fascination of recognising through the ever more transparent form of his beloved, the distances opened to his desire for unending possession.

How he would weep for whole nights with the longing to be himself shot through with such rays! But a woman loved, who yields, is still far from being a woman who loves. O nights without consolation, when his overflowing gifts came back to him piece-meal, and heavy with transience! How often he thought then of the troubadours who feared nothing more than to be granted what they asked! He gave all his possessions, inherited and acquired, not to have this experience. He wounded women with his gross payments, fearing from day to day lest they try to respond to his love. For he no longer had the hope of meeting the lover who should penetrate him utterly.

Even at the time when poverty terrified him every day with new hardships, when his head was the darling of misery and utterly worn bare, when ulcers opened all over his body like auxiliary eyes against the blackness of his tribulation, when he shuddered at the offal to which men had abandoned him because he was of the same nature with it; still even then, when he reflected, his greatest terror was lest anyone should respond to him. What were all these afflictions compared to the intense sadness of those embraces in which all was lost? Did one not wake with the feeling that no future remained? Did one not go about void of significance, without a right to danger? Had not one had to promise a hundred times not to die? Perhaps it was the stubbornness of this bitter memory, which came and came again and always kept itself a place, that enabled his life to endure amidst the filth. Finally he was found again. And not till then, not till the years of his shepherd's life, was his crowded past appeased.

Who shall describe what befell him then? What poet has the persuasive gift to reconcile the length of the days he now lived through with the brevity of life? What art is great enough to evoke simultaneously his thin, cloaked figure and the whole high spaciousness of his gigantic nights?

That was the time which began with his feeling himself a part of the universe and anonymous, like a lingering convalescent. He did not love, unless it were that he loved to live. The lowly affection of his sheep did not weigh upon him; like light falling through clouds it dispersed itself about him and gleamed softly on the meadows. In the innocent track of their hunger he strode silently across the pastures of the world. Strangers saw him on the Acropolis; and perhaps he was for a long time one of the shepherds in Les Baux, and saw the petrified age outlast that lofty race which, despite all its acquisition of sevens and threes, could not master the sixteen rays of its star. Or should I imagine him at Orange, leaning on the rustic triumphal arch? Should I see him in the spirit-haunted shade of Aliscamps as, among graves that stand open like the graves of those who have risen from the dead, his eyes pursue a dragon-fly?

It matters little, I see more than himself: I see his being which then began the long way of love to God — that silent, aimless labour. For he who had wanted to hold himself back for ever was once more dominated by his heart's increasing inability to be other than it was. And this time he hoped for a response. His whole nature, grown prescient and unerring in the long solitude, assured him that He of whom he now thought, knew how to love with a penetrating, radiant love. But while he longed to be loved at last so masterfully, his senses, accustomed to far distances, grasped the extreme remoteness of God. Nights came when he thought of flinging himself at Him through space; hours full of discovery, when he felt himself strong enough to plunge back to the earth and snatch it up on the stormy flood of his heart. He was like one who hears a noble language and feverishly undertakes to write in it. He had still to experience the dismay of discovering how difficult this language was. He was unwilling to believe at first that a long life might pass in learning to form the first short phrases of senseless exercises. He flung himself into this study like a runner in a race; but the density of what he had to master made him slacken his pace. Nothing more humiliating could be imagined than this apprenticeship. He had found the philosopher's stone, and now he was compelled ceaselessly to transmute the swiftly made gold of his happiness back again into the gross lead of patience. He who had come to be at home in universal space crawled like a worm in tortuous passages without outlet or direction. Now that he learned to love through so much labour and sorrow, it was shown him how negligible and unworthy all the love had been which he thought he had accomplished; how nothing could have come of it, since he had not begun to work at it and make it real.

During those years great changes took place in him. He almost forgot God in the hard task of drawing near Him, and all that he hoped perhaps to obtain from Him was *'sa patience de supporter une âme.'* Long ago he had detached himself from the accidents of fate to which men cling, but now even whatever of pleasure and pain were necessary lost their spicy aftertaste and became pure and nourishing to him. From the roots of his being there sprang the sturdy, evergreen plant of a fertile joy. He was wholly engrossed in learning to handle what constituted his inner life; he wanted to omit nothing, for he doubted not that his love dwelt and grew in all this. Indeed, his inward serenity went so far that he resolved to overtake the most important of those things which he had hitherto been unable to accomplish, the things he had simply allowed to slip past while he waited. Above all he thought of his childhood, which, the calmer his reflection, seemed to him more and more to have been unfulfilled; all its memories had about them the vagueness of premonitions, and that they were reckoned as past, made them almost part of the future. And to take all this once more, and this time in reality, upon himself — this was the reason he, estranged, turned home. We know not whether he remained; we only know that he returned.

Those who have told the story try at this point to remind us of the house as it looked then; for there only a short time has passed, a period easily reckoned; everyone in the house can say how long. The dogs have grown old, but they are still alive. It is said that one of them howled. The whole day's work is interrupted. Faces appear at the windows, faces that have aged and faces that have grown up, touchingly resembling one another. And in one quite old face, gone suddenly pale, recognition flashes. Recognition? Really only recognition? — Forgiveness? Forgiveness for what? — Love! My God, love!

But he, the person recognised, was so preoccupied that he had not been thinking of love, whether it might still exist. It is easy to understand how, of all that happened then, only this has been transmitted to us: his gesture, an unprecedented gesture that had never before been seen — the gesture of supplication, with which he threw himself at their feet, imploring them not to love him. Terrified and uncertain, they lifted him up. They interpreted his outburst in their own fashion, forgiving him. It must have been an indescribable relief to him that they all misunderstood him despite the desperate evidence of his attitude. Probably he was able to remain. For he recognised more clearly from day to day that the love of which they were so vain, and to which they secretly encouraged one another, did not concern him. He almost had to smile at their endeavours, and it was evident how little they could be thinking about him.

What did they know of him? He was now terribly difficult to love, and he felt that One alone was capable of loving him. But He was not yet willing.

END OF JOURNAL

PRINTED IN GREAT BRITAIN BY
LOWE AND BRYDONE PRINTERS LIMITED, LONDON, N.W.10